SINGLE

SINGLE and Feeling Good

Harold Ivan Smith

Abingdon Press

Nashville

SINGLE
and Feeling Good

Copyright © 1987 by Abingdon Press

All rights reserved.

This book is printed on acid-free paper.

Library of Congress Cataloging in Publication Data

SMITH, HAROLD IVAN

   Single.

   Bibliography: p.
   1. Single people. 2. Single people—Religious life.
   I. Title.
   HQ800.T67   1987   305'.90652   87-1799

ISBN 0-687-38552-0
(pbk.: alk. paper)

Scripture quotations unless otherwise noted are from the Revised Standard Version of the Bible, copyrighted 1946, 1952, © 1971, 1973 by the Division of Christian Education of the National Council of the Churches of Christ in the U.S.A., and used by permission.

Those marked NIV are from the Holy Bible, New International Version. Copyright © 1973, 1978, 1984, International Bible Society.

Quotations noted NEB are from The New English Bible. © the Delegates of the Oxford University Press and the Syndics of the Cambridge University Press 1961, 1970. Reprinted by permission.

Verses marked TLB are taken from The Living Bible, copyright © 1971 by Tyndale House Publishers, Wheaton, Ill. Used by permission.

Quotations marked KJV are from the King James Version of the Bible.

Excerpts on pages 19 and 61 are from Jason Towner, *Warm Reflections* (Nashville: Broadman Press, 1977). All rights reserved. Used by permission.

The words of the ad on page 41 are reprinted by permission of Beecham Cosmetics.

The quotation on pages 47-48 is from the February 19, 1982, issue of *Christianity Today* and is used by permission of the author Rosalie de Rosset.

MANUFACTURED BY THE PARTHENON PRESS AT
NASHVILLE, TENNESSEE, UNITED STATES OF AMERICA

This book is dedicated to an incredible woman—

> a single adult
> a dedicated teacher
> a compassionate soul
> a caring Christian
> an individual who has made a difference!

In her classroom and through watching her life, I first learned that singleness could be positive. She stretched my imagination, challenged my biases, and encouraged me to feel good about my singleness. With great respect, I dedicate this book to

Alice Cobb, Ph.D.

CONTENTS

COMMENTS————1

"IF IT'S ALL THE SAME TO YOU, I'D RATHER BE MARRIED."

But seek first his kingdom and his righteousness, and all these things will be yours as well (Matt. 6:33).

It's O.K. to want to be married.

"I want a man! I'm tired of all this singleness." The statement came from an attractive single adult, at the end of one of my seminars. Then she added, "I was made to be a wife!"

Initially, I wasn't anxious to agree. But, after thinking about it, I've decided that probably 95 percent of single adults want to get married—that is, in a general sort of way. Many young unmarrieds say, "Oh, I'm not single. I just haven't married yet."

That conclusion squares with new census figures. For individuals sixty-five or over in 1983 only 5.4 percent remained "never married," surprisingly down from 7.7 percent in 1970.

So, there's nothing wrong with wanting to marry. It's the American thing to do (or, some would argue, try). However, there are questions about how one goes about getting married.

I'm trying a new diet: *the best.* You can eat almost anything as long as it's *the best.* Suppose I've got the cookie-hungries. Well, I *could* go to the 7-Eleven store and plunk down my $1.49 and get a package of Oreos. Twenty minutes later the hungries are gone. That's one benefit of singleness. I can open the Oreo, lick out the vanilla, and throw away the chocolate wafers. But Oreos are store-bought, mass-produced cookies.

Four miles away is _____. The best cookies in the world. Their peanut butter ones are beyond description (no wonder: a thousand calories a bite).

There's nothing wrong with wanting a cookie. But, because of the best diet, I choose to defer gratification until I am on the Plaza and can get the best at _____.

Surprisingly, the diet works! Because I choose to wait for the best, my taste buds are not deluded with the ordinary.

I think the same is true of marriage. Are you willing to wait for the best?

A lot of "good" or "ordinary" potential mates are out there in Singleland. Remember your mother's advice on your shopping trips. "Now don't buy the first thing you see!" For the impatient, the decision to marry may be the first step toward an ironic consequence: the divorce court. Their anxiety is replaced by the disillusionment of recognizing Prince or Princess Charming is an imposter.

How many times have you been asked, "Don't you want to get married?" as if getting married is no more difficult than placing a classified. One woman responded to a nosy questioner, "I've observed your marriage and decided I could do a lot better by waiting!"

Impatience has ruined too many relationships. How many single adults ask as they meet someone, "O Lord let *this* be the one." How many have been hastily disposed of because of a poor first impression? Others were discarded when the veneer wore thin.

You're positive you'd be happier if you were married.

But a million marrieds woke up this morning convinced they would be happier if they were single.

I have been accused of not believing in marriage, of being against marriage. Some people have mentioned Paul's note that in the last days would come those who preached against marriage (I Tim. 4:1-3). I'm not one of those. I believe in marriage, but I also believe in giving singleness a fair chance. Both are legitimate life-styles; neither is less or more honorable.

In this book, I'm going to share some insights. You don't have to "buy" everything or anything, but I would hope that you will seriously think about the ideas, that you will be "teachable."

From the start I'll admit that singleness is *not* always wonderful! But neither is marriage. Both estates have agonies and ecstacies; highs and lows.

So, even if you hate singleness in general and yours in particular, this book can help you survive until Prince/cess Charming arrives on a white horse to whisk you away.

There are also ideas that will help you *thrive* as well as survive.

For many singleness is an exhibition season; for a few it is a permanent season; for some it is an interlude. Whatever, the common ingredient is your attitude. You decide, Will I *survive* or *thrive* my singleness?

"WHAT'S GETTING INTO ALL THESE PEOPLE?"

House and wealth are inherited from [parents] but a prudent [mate] is from the Lord (Prov. 19:14).

The family crisis is not new.

Family has become an emotion-charged word in contemporary American society. Politicians, television

11

evangelists, commentators all address the family crisis. Look at these quotations and try to guess the date.

> The foundation of marriage is, of course, the very foundation of our social organization and all influences that affect that institution are of vital concern to the people of the whole country. There is widespread conviction that (there is) . . . a diminishing regard for the sanctity of the marriage relation.[1]

My guess is ___*1920*___.

> The family in its old sense is disappearing from our land, and not only our free institutions are threatened, but the very existence of our society is endangered.[2]

My guess is ___*1850*___.

> The growth . . . has come, in some measure, as a result of the increased freedom of women. When women could get a living only through some man, a husband meant income. Now that a woman can give up her husband and get her own living, she has more respect for herself and expects more.[3]

My guess is ___*1965*___.

> It is high time that the press, the pulpit, and every other avenue open to the public mind, were alive on this subject, presenting, reiterating, and enforcing the sanctity, integrity and perpetuity of marriage.[4]

My guess is ___*1815*___.

How did you guess? Here are the correct years:

1909   1859   1907   1889

Clearly, the family crisis has been around longer than we have.

Throughout American history, the excuse, "I couldn't find anyone" annoyed many American leaders.

The following statement is from *Single Blessedness*, "If Brigham Young, wearing throat whiskers could assemble between thirty-five and forty at one time, how pitiful becomes the alibi of the modern maverick that he has never managed to arrive at any sort of marital arrangement."[5]

But, let's face it. There are visible single adults. California had a two-term bachelor governor; the mayor of New York is unmarried. While nine out of ten Americans marry, 10 percent accounts for a lot of single adults either "blessed" or "unblessed."

Of course there is a battle over what to call them. Americans have long used the terms "old maid," "spinster," or "unclaimed blessing." However, there were no such derogatory terms for males who did not marry.

Many conservatives reject the notion of referring to the widowed or divorced as single. Many people are frightened by singleness. They see it as a rejection of societal norms and expectations. In 1957, when researchers asked individuals what they thought of persons who did not marry, 53 percent responded that such persons were either sick or immoral, and probably too selfish or neurotic to marry. Twenty years later, that attitude was expressed by only 33 percent of the survey.[6]

The nuclear family (composed of father, mother, and offspring) now comprises only 34.4 percent of the American population if one includes the millions of blended families.

The treatment of the single adult is handicapped by myths. In American society, there exists

> a fierce nostalgia for some lost golden age of the family. . . . Many people, faced with the obvious discrepancy between the realities of today's family life and the model (the sentimental) refuse to give up the idea of domestic perfection, and project it back into the past.[7]

Thus, "if only" we could get back to the Waltons. Noll and Hatch agree with Jerome Kagan "that every age has favorite myths about the child and family which it regards as obviously true." However, "the idea that a more-or-less generally Christian culture prevailed in America until recent times lowers the guard of Christians to distinguish what is truly biblical from that which is merely part of their cultural heritage."[8]

"What we need is a rebirth of commitment" argue the conservatives who want you to accept *their* definition of family as *the* norm. Rather than asking why people do not get married, I would offer Ellen Rothman's analysis of why people get married. Her list also explains why people get divorced and why some people fear marriage.

Real reasons people marry

- For a meal ticket
- To have a housekeeper, secretary, parent
- To say that they did
- To prove something
- For readily available sex
- To avoid loneliness
- To please their parents
- For money
- For prestige
- For power
- To further their career
- To make potential or business alliances
- To get even with an old lover
- To get out of the parental home
- To become a U.S. citizen
- To obtain a father/mother for their children
- Because they think it's their only opportunity
- To have children
- Because someone else loves them
- Because of pressure from family or society
- Because they hate themselves[9]

The list is sobering and should be shared the next time someone wants to know why you haven't married. Of course, some single adults respond in humor. One woman laughs, "No man deserves as much love as I could give!"

Consider the psychological reasons for remaining unmarried which Dorothy Payne identified.

- Fear of intimacy and love
- Dislike of [the opposite sex]
- Strong wish for independence
- Unwillingness to live with a less than perfect situation or person
- Unrealistic dreams about relationships
- Unrealistic expectations of [the opposite sex]
- Unwillingness to share time and energy
- Qualities that intimidate [the opposite sex] . . .
- Sexual attraction to [the same sex]
- Lack of social skills in conversation and dating
- Memories of earlier difficulties with [opposite sex]
- Uncertainty of what one wants[10]

But a major reason is "because I don't want to." I think the current slowdown to the altar should be applauded. Many experts do not interpret the high divorce rate as a rejection of marriage. Rather, the remarriage rate indicates that there was a rejection of a specific partner or situation.

"EVERYONE OUGHT TO BE MARRIED!"

Marriage should be honored by all (Heb. 13:4 NIV).

One is a whole number.

"Love and marriage, go together like a horse and carriage" are words from an old song. Family was the major unit of the Bible. Since all males were expected to marry so that the promise of God to Abraham could be fulfilled (see Gen. 5:4-9), there was no word for bachelor in Hebrew. Marriage modeled the relationship between God and his people.

Though God's original design was for monogamy, from Abraham on there are traces of polygamy, which was not forbidden, but was necessitated by infertility. Marriage in the Old Testament served for the procreation of offspring and thus apparently justified polygamy. No restrictions were placed on age, although somewhere between fourteen and twenty was apparently common. A girl was considered eligible for marriage soon after her first menstruation.

In the patriarchal age, it was the duty of the father to arrange a marriage for his son. Abraham made his chief servant swear that he would not secure a wife for Isaac from among the Canaanites (Gen. 24:3), and Judah "took a wife for Er his first-born" (Gen. 38:6). One exception was Ishmael. It was his mother Hagar who secured an Egyptian wife for him (Gen. 21:21).

However, sometimes the man chose but his parents negotiated as in the case of Shechem (Gen. 34:4) and Samson (Judg. 14:2). But apparently some men, such as Esau, married against their parents' wishes. "When Esau was forty years old, he married Judith . . . and also Basemath . . . . They were a source of grief to Isaac and Rebekah" (Gen. 26:34-35, NIV). Rebekah must have been a fascinating mother-in-law, because she said to Isaac, "I'm disgusted with living because of these Hittite women [Esau's wives]. If Jacob takes a wife from among the women of this land, from Hittite women like these, my life will not be worth living" (Gen. 27:46, NIV).

There were no formal wedding ceremonies although Genesis hints at the custom of a wedding feast, at which the bride was given to the husband. This was called "taking of the bride." "So Laban brought together all the people of the place and gave a feast. But when evening came, he took his daughter Leah and gave her to Jacob" (Gen. 29:22-23, NIV).

Verse 23 indicates that the couple was escorted to the bridal chamber. This is also suggested in apocryphal literature (Tob. 7:16-17; 8:1). Before intercourse prayer was offered for the husband and wife (Tob. 8:4).

Some groups, such as the Essenes, rejected marriage. In fact, they may have regarded all sexual relations as unclean. Paul warned about those who would forbid marriage (I Tim. 4:3).

In the Gospels, marriage and the wedding are the allegory of Christ's relationship to his bride, the church (II Cor. 11:2). Jesus is pictured as the bridegroom and the hope is for that promised marriage feast of the Lamb (Rev. 19:7).

If the Gospel writers were writing today, perhaps they would have to seek another allegory because of the low repute, shallowness, and temporality of present-day marriage.

The Old Testament looked at marriage from the man's point of view: a woman was his possession through which he gained offspring.

In the New Testament, a man's rights gave way to shared rights. However, this is subject to interpretation and is cause for the emotional battle on submission of women. No small number choose to quote Ephesians 5:22-23: "Wives, submit to your husbands as to the Lord. For the husband is the head of the wife as Christ is the head of the church" (NIV). This has been used to justify all sorts of weird and aberrant interpretations and behaviors. Yet, Paul did not stop at verse 23. He continued, "Husbands, love your wives, just as Christ loved the church" (v. 25).

The traditional marriage ceremony indicates that marriage is "not to be entered into unadvisedly, but reverently, discreetly, and in the fear of God." However, people get married for all sorts of reasons:

1. to legitimize sexual relations
2. to get away from bad home situations
3. to follow their peers

4. to gain personal security
5. to escalate a stagnant relationship

And some have not "fallen in love," but were "pushed" into marriage by overanxious parents.

Marriage is meant to be a permanent commitment. In the romantic nostalgia of the wedding, that seems easy to affirm. Yet, the high divorce rate indicates that it has become easier to suggest, "Well, if it doesn't work out, we can always get a divorce." Such an attitude ignores the deep trauma of separation and divorce which lacerates the soul and spirit.

Marriage was not designed for shoring-up sagging egos.

Parents use plastic colored eggs to teach children size and color coordination. A child takes half an egg shell and by random keeps trying to fit it to the other half. Eventually, by trial and error, the child succeeds.

Sometimes, single adults feel the same way—like half an egg shell until someone comes along. I do not become whole in marriage; I become whole in relationship to Jesus Christ. "For in Christ all the fullness of the Deity lives in bodily form, and you have been given fullness in Christ" (Col. 2:9-10, NIV) or as the KJV translates, you "are complete in him."

So marriage becomes the union of two whole individuals. God's design is for a rich, growing love to become a witness to a world that has grown skeptical of the claims of marriage.

Furthermore, a strong component in the marriage is for both partners to be believers. "Do not be yoked together with unbelievers" (II Cor. 6:14a, NIV) has been the continuous tradition of the church. A Christian marriage cannot be between one Christian and one non-believer. Paul asked, "What does a believer have in common with an unbeliever?" (II Cor. 6:15b, NIV).

In *Warm Reflections,* I contend that a marriage becomes Christian sometime after the ceremony,

    when stress and strain
       have tarnished the romantic notions
       and a couple is far wiser about each other;
    when they find they want to continue
       to be in love, to be aware, and to be husband and wife.

    A Christian marriage is a daily commitment that realizes
       that vows made at a flower-lined altar
       are only as good as those made at the altars of everyday
        life.

And a Christian concept of marriage realizes that the vows made at a flower-lined altar are only as good as those made at the altar of the heart, daily.

BACKGROUND————2

WHAT ABOUT TRADITION?

You have let go of the commands of God and are holding on to the traditions of men" (Mark 7:8, NIV).

It's hard to hold onto the baby when you throw out the bath water!

Most of the attitudes on singleness in the church reflect our interpretation of Paul's teachings. Convinced that the second coming of Christ was imminent, Paul wrote, "because of the present crisis" (I Cor. 7:26, NIV), everyone *should* remain in the state in which he was called, whether married or single. However, Paul left no doubt that he preferred singleness.

But Paul's days passed. Slowly the church began interpreting what Jesus and Paul had said. That both had been unmarried encouraged enthusiasm for mandatory celibacy.

The early church took root in a sexually explosive social setting. Male and female prostitutes worked in the Corinthian temples; in Greece, homosexuality was common. The Essenes preached against marriage. Had Paul and the Apostles remained in Palestine, we might have had a different Christian tradition. But as the faithful migrated, they encountered a pagan world view with radically different ideas on marriage and sexuality.

The ascetics were strong in the Western world. Epicurus declared: "The wise man will not fall in love . . . [and] will not marry and raise a family. Occasionally, he will marry owing to special circumstances in his life."[1]

Jesus, however, suggested the opposite: a man might remain single due to special circumstances in his life (Matt. 9:11-13). The intellectuals in ancient Greece thought sex "a nuisance, or at best, an appetite likely to interfere with the conduct of life according to the Golden Mean."[2] When Diogenes was asked the proper time to marry, he replied, "For a young man not yet; for an old man, never at all."

The early church took literally Galatians 3:28, "There is no such thing as Jew and Greek, slave and freeman, male and female" (NEB) and added "as married or single." After all, they had Jesus' words that we would not marry in heaven (Matt. 22:30). Since the eternal state would be sexless, the best preparation for the heavenly bliss was to begin celibacy now.[3]

Origen counseled men and women at all hours of the night and wanted nothing to compromise his witness. So, he castrated himself and justified his actions with Scripture. "If your hand causes you to sin, cut it off; it is better for you to enter life maimed than with two hands to go to hell" (Mark 9:43).[4]

Augustine, one of the most influential thinkers, addressed such issues in his *Confessions*. While involved with a mistress, he became engaged to another woman, dismissing the mistress only to become involved with yet another woman. His singleness left him distressed. He prayed, "Lord, make me pure—but not now."

It was not until he was thirty-two that he accepted Christianity as the only means to discipline his unmanageable sexual desires. Augustine recommended celibacy,

21

obviously aware that if his advice were taken, "human history would be quickly ended." Some perceived his teaching as a means of "forcing God's hands so as to usher in the end of the world."[5]

For those without discipline, marriage was the *only* practical answer. Some church leaders questioned marriage. Ambrose quipped, "Married people ought to blush when they consider the lives they live." Jerome suggested that any man who loved his wife too much was an adulterer. Jerome may have been the originator of marriage jokes: "I do not condemn wedlock. I would like everyone to take a wife who cannot manage to sleep alone because he gets frightened at night."[6] Moreover, since sex was nonexistent in heaven, he urged: "Let us husbands cherish our wives, and let our souls cherish their bodies, so that wives may be turned into husbands and bodies into souls, . . . so let us also . . . begin to be right now on earth what has been promised we shall be in heaven."[7]

Aquinas identified two levels of morality: the high road for celibates (singles) and the *low* road for the marrieds (an interesting reversal of today's assessment). Heterosexual generation must have been ordained by God, Aquinas reasoned, because another male would have been a better worker.

Slowly, a group of norms emerged. The female was clearly "inferior" to the male. Eve and *all* her daughters had the sentence of God upon them. Some priests fled from a woman as quickly as from the devil. Benedict, upset with sexual thoughts, stripped naked and wrestled a briar bush until his skin was torn. A priest could receive up to one hundred lashes just for speaking alone to a woman. In many churches and cemeteries, women were banned.[8]

The church pointed to the ceremonial impurity of females in the Old Testament for support. Eventually, "married couples were instructed to abstain from intercourse for three days before coming to Holy Communion, in order that they might be in a proper spiritual condition to receive the sacrament."[9] As the church wrote rules and devised punishment for the weak, a double standard developed. Expectations were tougher on the clergy than laity, on the woman than the man, on the single than the married.[10]

Eventually, celibacy was enforced on all clergy. However, the standard had an expedient effect. The Papacy could become a political force only through a group of men whose loyalty was solely to the church. Celibacy prevented the inheritance of property and broke up many political alliances based on marriage.

Many men escaped the real world by entering monasteries; women became "brides of Christ" in convents. Even widows joined the convents. Ironically, most discovered that the problems of the outside world were present within the walled worlds. Although craftsmanship and scholarship were at a high point, the separation emphasized an unrealistic discipline of sexuality.

Then Martin Luther stepped forward. He argued that marriage provided an opportunity for spiritual growth and an alternative to the embarrassing problems of priests with illegitimate children and common-law wives. He refuted Aquinas' notion "that no person of spiritual refinement could frequent the marketplace or the marriage bed."[11]

Celibacy, Luther argued, challenged biblical teaching and man's natural instincts. While sex was sinful, in marriage "God overlooked it." "Had God consulted me about it," Luther boasted, "I should have advised Him to continue the generation of the species by fashioning human beings out of clay, as Adam was made!"[12]

Luther helped several women escape from a convent in 1525 and arranged marriages for all but one. When he could not find a husband for Katherine von Bora, he married her himself. In his view, one wife was as good as another.

Another influential thinker was Erasmus, an illegitimate son of a priest, who lamented that too many priests were appropriately addressed as "father." Erasmus rejected the notion that priests could not marry because Jesus had not married. Humans, he countered, could not imitate Jesus in every detail (for example, the virgin birth). However, Erasmus had no tolerance for those who married to challenge tradition or the "horde of priests among whom chastity is rare." He believed the church directly profited from such because the bishops taxed the concubines of the priests.[13]

His follower, Zwingli, fathered a child and admitted that he could not remain chaste for more than a year at a time. However, he took pride that he had never seduced a nun or a virgin. He petitioned for the right of clergy to marry.

John Calvin's *Institutes of the Christian Religion* had quite an impact. Calvin preached that marriage had two major functions: procreation and "remedying sin." Still, Calvin had difficulty with sensual pleasure. He counseled husbands to approach their wives "with delicacy and propriety." He eventually married a widow, Idelette de Bure Stordeur in 1539 and became a stepparent to her children. Calvin attacked priests. "Disgraceful lusts rage among them, so that hardly one in ten lives chastely; and in monasteries, the least of the evils is ordinary fornication."[14]

Calvin also chided those who teased about marriage. Such humor, in Calvin's thinking, originated in "Satan's workshop." Any attack on marriage was an insult to God. For the majority of people "God not only permits but positively commands marriage, and any who resist matrimony are fighting against God. It is, therefore, a foolish imagination that celibacy is a virtue."[15]

While the Reformation altered the perspective of many on marriage, the period provided a framework for the moralism and legalism of the Puritans. Later came the Victorians who made prudery a virtue. Layers of clothing disguised the female anatomy; sex was acceptable only for the preservation of the race and to temper the "beast" in the nature of human males.

Single adults must understand that the church will not easily abandon its perspective of marriage as "the norm." Celibacy and singleness were recognized as the "high roads" for centuries; however, the excesses of that period have not been forgotten.

It is hoped that this gives you some idea of the weave of the fabric that shapes the church's tradition on single-ness. We're fortunate to live in this historical time period rather than the previous ones.

WHAT ABOUT HISTORY?

And by faith he still speaks, even though he is dead (Heb. 11:4c, NIV).

Single adults have been movers and shakers!

"The hand that rocks the cradle rules the world" is a popular American folk myth, as is the saying, "Behind every successful man, is a woman!" Single adults have had an equally significant impact on our history and culture. Admittedly, the American colonists had a strong commit-ment to marriage. A colony needed people. There were two ways to gain this commodity: through immigration and through birth. Moreover, those born in the colonies would have less allegiance to the mother country. Early colonists thought "it was a man's duty to marry; it was a woman's reason for existence." Therefore, every settler's ambition was to get a mate and some land and to reap the blessings of God, i.e., children and crops and profits.

In colonial days the family was an economic produc-tion unit; a big family meant more crops could be produced. William Byrd II of Virginia joked, "An old maid or old bachelor are as scarce among us and reckoned as ominous as a blazing star." He laughed that his nineteen-year-old daughter "was the most ancient virgin" he knew.[16]

William Penn, founder of Pennsylvania, urged his colonists to become "a nursery of people." He introduced a bill in the legislature "to compel the young men to marry." His law would have been hard to enforce since there were so many more men than women. In New England, bachelors could not choose their own living accommodations. The court assigned them to families where they could be "supervised."[17]

Some colonies only granted land to married men. Maryland taxed bachelors, light wines, and billiard tables. Yet some men reasoned that paying the bachelor's tax was still cheaper than maintaining a family. The College of William and Mary hired only single males to teach and paid them low salaries. If a professor married he was immediately fired.

One Dutch colonist said that bachelors reminded him of rogue elephants, "walking around like ghosts."

In some areas, because of the shortage of white women, males lived with Indian women, arguing that such liaisons built closer ties with the Indians.

North Carolina editors had little use for unmarried women.

> An old maid is one of the most cranky, ill-natured maggoty, peevish, conceited, disagreeable, hypocritical, fretful, noisy, gibing, canting, censorious, out-of-the-way, never-to-be-pleased, good-for-nothing creatures. . . . In short, an old maid enters the world to take up room, not to make room for others.[18]

Colonists wrote back to unmarried siblings and cousins to come to America where they would have a better chance to marry. However, it must be remembered that colonial life was cruel. Many women died in childbirth, after only a few years of married life.

But some of the colonists were spinsters. Georgia granted 450 acres to Ann Andrews in 1758. Yet, Deborah Holmes was denied land. Instead, the governors gave her four bushels of corn saying it "would be a bad precedent to keep house alone."[19] Margaret Brent was a capable estate administrator in Maryland.

Naturally, in matters of love, there was cultural confusion because of the conflict between old world traditions and new world realities. Greetje Waemans petitioned the authorities that Daniel de Silk "be condemned to legally marry me." De Silk explained that he had been drunk and was not responsible. He was ordered to be more careful in his affections.

In another instance, Francois Soliel, a New Amsterdam gunsmith, declared that he would rather live among the Indians than "marry the Fair Rose whom he had left to droop neglected."[20]

By the time of the Revolution, serial marriages were quite common since so many women died in childbirth. And when a husband died, our forefathers preferred the widow to remarry rather than to be on public assistance. Most widows were snapped up. One New Hampshire governor married a widow six days after her husband's death. In Virginia, a funeral feast for the first husband turned into a wedding feast for the second!

Single men preferred widows. For one thing, the woman's fertility had been proven. Second, with the widow came land and perhaps children to work the land. Benjamin Franklin quipped, "A rich widow is the only kind of second-hand goods that always sells at prime cost." Furthermore, he advised one young man: "Marry immediately! Take an old woman . . . they are so grateful!"[21]

Elizabeth Murray, a Scot, is an example of the unmarried woman proprietor. When she came to America in 1749 to visit her brother, she brought with her a supply of millinery and dry goods. When her ship docked in Boston, she decided to stay there and open a shop.

Single men were suspicious of novel-reading women. John Quincy Adams danced with one maid and observed, "She . . . has read too many novels, which renders her manners rather fanatical and affected."[22]

The death of Jane McCrea, a single woman, had a major impact on both sides of the ocean. Her death aroused strong anti-British feelings.

However, the Revolution challenged the perception of marriage partners. Gradually, potential bridegrooms came to be evaluated by their future possibilities rather than by their past. Women participated in the Revolution and assumed that they would be rewarded. Two single women voted in New Jersey in October, 1787. However, the issue was hotly debated in Virginia. In all states, married women were denied the right to vote.

The Revolution opened the western lands to pioneers. Thousands of men found brides and moved West to stake their claims.

Deborah Sampson was awarded a pension for service during the Revolution; she had disguised herself as a male in order to serve. When Emily Geiger, a courier, was captured by the British, she refused to be searched by a male. While a female guard was located, Emily "ate" the message.[23] In North Carolina, women pledged to refuse any suitor who had not answered the call to military service.

During the war, Francis Asbury organized the American Methodist Church, relying primarily on his unmarried circuit riders. Many of these men rode twenty to fifty miles per day on horseback, often preaching five times a day. As the American West expanded, Asbury asked preachers to follow the settlers, preferably men who did not have families. Often romance hampered the Bishop's plan. He once complained that women and the devil were getting all his preachers.

Luther Rice aggressively organized the Baptists. He had been the first American missionary. On April 10,

1814, Rice addressed Congress on the needs of foreign missions and raised $87 in a freewill offering. He later helped organize the Triennial Convention which later became the American and Southern Baptist Conventions. To educate the clergy, he founded Columbian College in Washington which later became George Washington University.[24]

After the Revolution there was a test of the conviction "All men are created equal." The debate had an effect on choice of marriage partners as well as political rights.

ON THE AMERICAN FRONTIER

On the frontier, Americans married young, as early as fifteen or sixteen years old. Indeed, twenty-seven-year-old grandmothers were common in North Carolina. One German chuckled, "As soon as a boy has $100 he thinks of marrying." Parents gave a horse, some crude farm implements, and seeds as wedding presents.[25]

In this period, a woman went from a bed in her father's house to a bed in her husband's cabin or tent. A Western woman did not have to be beautiful to have suitors. Her cooking, modesty, and skillful management were highly valued. A Western man was evaluated on his ability to work, his health, and his knowledge of some trade or business.

However, some women were prized because they owned land and/or slaves or stood to inherit such. One Mississippi writer noted that the unpardonable sin for a southern woman was poverty. One Tennessee groom praised his wife's "excellent qualities" which included "a good piece of land about ten or twelve miles from Nashville."[26]

The New York Advocate in 1819 questioned why there were so many old damsels and bachelors. The editor blamed "the extravagance of fashion" as one factor that frightened men away from marriage. How sad that "old bachelors marry to get nurses!"[27]

George Rogers Clark, a general, had deeply loved Teresa de Loyala. Because of war claims the government rejected, he was unable to honorably marry a woman "accustomed to all the luxuries of wealth." Eventually, she entered a monastery in Italy. Newspapers blamed the "high cost of living" for the decline in marriage.[28]

Soon, authors and humorists attacked the unmarried. One proposed that a committee of old maids confront bachelors and "demand of them their reasons for remaining single."

The anonymous author of *Single Blessedness* fired back this quick retort:

> Old maids have no right to make such a demand. Why men remain unmarried is nobody's concern but their own. And they are not bound to treat any body civilly who questions them on the subject. . . . Any unmarried man would do well to get angry at such an insulting interference in his personal affairs.[29]

David Dammer's play, *Single Life: A Comedy* was popular with Western audiences. One character, Narcissus Boss, a "self-loving bachelor," was confronted by a "singing spinster," Kitty Skylark,

Skylark: "Oh, sir, I am afraid you admire yourself too much to bestow a thought of regard on one of us poor women."
Boss: "I shall never marry until I discover perfection."
Skylark: "Then you will find grey hairs hanging over your temples, before you obtain that object."
Boss: "Then I'll die a bachelor!"[30]

Coy, his fellow bachelor added, "All the rest of the world begins with love and finishes with hating. We bachelors will be wiser by beginning with hate and, perhaps, ending with love."

Honor blocked many marriages. Missionary Henry Martyn's love, Lydia, could not marry him since she had been previously engaged to another man and did not feel free to marry Martyn until the first man died.[31]

James Buchanan's engagement was broken by his fiancée. Ten days later she died. Buchanan confessed, "I may sustain the shock of her death, but I feel that happiness has fled from me, forever." Ironically, his depression after her death led his friends to secure a congressional nomination for him[32] as a diversion to his grief. He later became president of the United States.

A bachelor by the name of Abraham Lincoln wrote, "I can never be satisfied with anyone who would be blockheaded enough to have me."[33] But Mary Todd changed Lincoln's mind.

Stephen F. Austin, the Texas pioneer, never married. "The affection and loyalty that most men lavish upon their families he gave unstintingly to the welfare and happiness of Texas colonists," wrote his biographer. Austin declared: "The Prosperity of Texas has been the object of my labors, the idol of my existence."[34]

In the South, single men often consorted sexually with slaves. Often fathers arranged their wills so that sons inherited money or land only upon marriage. Unmarried women were expected to live with parents or with older, married siblings. Described as "forlorn damsels who make the midnight air echo with their plaintive bewailings," single women worked as governesses or maids. Many were considered an "extra pair of hands that didn't have to be paid" and were exploited "for the sake of the family."[35]

However, in the North, single women were actively recruited to work in the New England mills. Besides, there was a severe shortage of males in the East and marriage had to be delayed. Working offered women a chance to build dowries and thereby improve their chances of marriage. Lowell, a mill owner, explained to fathers of middle and low classes that unmarried daughters could contribute to rather than drain family incomes. He argued, "After a few years of labor in the mills, the women will be better wives and mothers." However, many of these women remained unmarried; their incomes financed a brother's education at Dartmouth or Yale. By 1820, New York City had 118 women (ages 16-26) for every 100 men; Philadelphia, 123 per 100; and Boston, 127 per 100. Gradually, these women were convinced to "go west."[36]

Single women who were Rachels in the Atlantic states migrated to the West and became Leahs. Many went west as schoolteachers under the inspiration and direction of Catharine Beecher, who was known to be "unable to submit to the will of God" and equally hesitant to submit to matrimony. Beecher saw these school marms as "educational missionaries." Thus, she legitimized teaching as a career for women.[37]

Strong leaders during this period were South Carolina spinster sisters Sarah and Angelina Grimké. They freed their slaves and moved north and became active speakers in the abolition movement. Sarah's book, *Slavery as It Is* sold over 100,000 copies and influenced Harriet Beecher Stowe to write *Uncle Tom's Cabin*. The Grimké sisters also promoted feminism.[38]

Many single adults, particularly in the West, used their single season as a time to seek their own destiny. They accumulated land and cattle and worked to tame the wilderness. The women who went west "civilized" the society. Still marriage was expected by most people.

BUILDING A SUCCESSFUL IDENTITY

While they were stoning him, Stephen prayed, "Lord Jesus, receive my spirit" (Acts 7:59, NIV).

The difference between what I am and what I become is what I do!

What can singles do to achieve a successful single adult identity? First, we must face our singleness. There are times when I do not like being unmarried. In one sense, I regret that someone made a decision that forced me to become single again.

Single adults often fail to understand that it is not so much what happens to us as how we choose to respond. So we may sob/wonder, "God, when are things going to get better?" But we have a lot to do with the answer.

I have to deal with the now, the me that I am. I have to face reality: I am a single adult and I have potentialities. I almost want to shout the chant of Jesse Jackson: "I am *somebody!*"

Many single adults have the notion that one of these days they are going to *discover* their single adult identity. You will not *discover* your identity. You *decide!* A successful single adult identity, an image, is always a decision.

Second, express and work through negative feelings. I don't have problems with people who have negative self-images, per se. What bothers me are those who have cosmetic images.

You need to express and work through your negative feelings. Be sure that they are *yours* and not borrowed or imposed. It is too easy for me to put old cassettes on my mental tape deck and sabotage my day or weekend or life.

Some of us would never lie down and let someone take a whip to us, but we beat ourselves with self-accusations. Express and work through your negative feelings. If it is someone else's cassette, get rid of it. Instead, listen to those positive aspects within you. You can grow and stretch. You have potential.

Third, separate the changeable from the unchangeable. There are some things about me that I cannot change. For instance, I am losing my hair and that really bugs me! How am I going to find a mate when my hair is gone? Don't women want to run their fingers through a man's hair (or have I watched one too many shampoo commercials)? I am not going to be able to do a lot about my hair. It's just going to be that way. It runs in the gene pool.

But there are other parts of me that I can change. For instance, my weight. I used to weigh 275 pounds (I had big bones!). I rationalized that I had always been heavy, but I rejected responsibility. I blamed my mother. It was all her fault, because she had those after-school snacks ready every day.

When I married, guess who I blamed? I tried all the crazy diets and fads. But my divorce brought me face to face with responsibility. I had to assume control of my weight. When I accepted responsibility, it made a difference on the scales.

The difference between what I am and what I become is what I do. I typed that phrase on a note card and taped it to my bathroom mirror. I still need to be reminded that I cause my weight. There are some things I cannot honestly change and some that I can. It's important for me to admit that reality and live redemptively.

You must accept responsibility.

Ten years ago I understood that for the first time in my life there was no one to look after me. It was not what my wife did to me in a North Carolina courtroom. It was what I chose to do with the rest of my life.

Consider a meaningful passage of scripture. Things were not going well for Stephen. You might paraphrase Judith Viorst to suggest he was having "a terrible, horrible, no-good, very bad day." This man of faith was being stoned to death. Death by stoning was a slow, painful death. Yet, Stephen prayed: "Lord Jesus, receive my spirit." Stephen wouldn't let the stones influence his attitude. That's courage.

All of us can restate his words, "Lord Jesus, receive my spirit/my attitude about my singleness. Help me become the person you want me to be." Not put on another person's armor or adopt someone else's agenda but be the unique *me* I was created to be.

Shaping an identity is a tough assignment. It means resisting the cultural pressure that squeezes us into its mold.

But remember, identity is your decision.

Humorist Carl Haney was right when he said, *"You* are the only one who can be you and get it right!"

LIFE-STYLE

Watch your life and doctrine closely (I Tim. 4:16a, NIV).

What I am speaks louder than what I say.

The one charateristic of singlehood that stirs the envy of married people is freedom. Many people have explained their divorce by saying, "I wanted my freedom."

However, that stirs a hint of animosity. Such freedom is perceived by many to be a lack of commitment or responsibility. The same people ask, "When are you going *to settle down* and get married?" The classification "swinging single" further illustrates this attitude.

Again, life-style is influenced by attitudes. Jesus declared that he had come that single adults might "have life and have it abundantly" (John 10:10). However, several alternative life-styles adopted by single adults block the abundant life-style.

Ark Thinking. Family is a significant theme in the Old Testament. Family is reflected in the genealogies and long lists of names which frequently appear. For Jews immortality was assured through the continuation of the seed, generation after generation, so every Jew was expected to marry and have as many children as possible. This Jewish influence has shaped evangelical thinking that everyone ought to get (and remain) married. If you aren't married, you are believed to be a half-person.

However, the concept of the nuclear family is not found in the New Testament. Indeed, the New Testament question is not, Are you married or single? but, Are you his? Jesus taught that marriage was a temporal thing (Matt. 22:30).

Who would have suggested to Corrie ten Boom, "O you half-person! If only you had had a family of your own!" Corrie ten Boom didn't wait for Prince Charming to appear. Corrie changed the world as a Kingdom-seeker.

Ark thinkers rephrase that childhood prayer, "Now I lay me down to sleep . . . if I should die before I marry."

Ash Thinking. We live in an age of success-obsession. Everyone is expected to be a success. Some of us know more about failure than success. We know the taste and smell of ashes. We have lain in the ashes; we have had our world crumble and tumble. Whether a death of a mate or fiancée, a divorce, the break-up of an engagement, a firing, we have felt the singe of disappointment. Some of us have watched from inside as the roof caved in.

Scripture promises that God "lifts the needy from the ash heap; he seats them with princes" (I Sam. 2:8a, NIV). While I cannot testify to that with total accuracy because I have never eaten with a prince, I can assure you of the accuracy of the first phrase.

That's why the story of Jesus healing the demoniac challenges me. The demoniac lived in the tombs. I meet a lot of single adults who smell nice, drive nice cars, make big bucks but "live in the tombs." Jesus healed the demoniac; Jesus longs to heal us today.

Jesus wants to help us in the midst of our messes and disappointments. Our theology has to work in our messes.

It is possible to find in the ashes of yesterday the nutrients for tomorrow's dreams.

Ape Thinking. Many single adults are into "the latest." They are celebrity conscious. In the most recent Olympics, the media used "stop frame," that one mini-second frozen on the camera. We could grasp the agony, the ecstasy. That is the way many single adults react to celebrities. We see only portions of their lives. We seldom see their bad times. But Mike Yaconelli noted, "We compare the perfections of these celebrities to our imperfections and we get discouraged, or worse yet, we put the celebrity on a pedestal and expect them to have the answers to all of life's problems."

Evangelicals often refuse to give up their worship of celebrities. Mike Yaconelli says: "There seems to be this unquenchable longing to hope with all our hearts that someone is able to live this Christian life the way it is supposed to be lived. We can't live that way, but surely Chuck Swindoll, or Amy Grant, or Joni can. Please God tell us it's true."[1]

Ape thinking offers 1, 2, 3s or instant solutions. Thus the gospel is adapted to contemporary living.

Ape-thinking single adults race to the *next* seminar, the *next* conference, buy the *next* book or cassette, hoping they will find the answers. No wonder some end up on Oregon hillsides with religious gurus.

Ask Thinking. To single adults in the ask-thinking life-style, God is the cosmic, eternal Santa Claus, the divine mail order catalog, a type of room service, as long as they know the secret code word.

Prayer has thus become "give me." Some single adults think they have to talk God into giving. In *My Utmost for His Highest* (Dodd, Mead, 1935), Oswald Chambers suggested that "we look upon prayer as a means of getting things for ourselves." However, "the Bible teaches that prayer is getting to know God himself."

Some single adults have concluded that their spiritual gift is receiving. They are like Ebenezer Scrooge, on Christmas Eve, counting their loot. The Word insists, "Give, and it will be given to you." And with the measure we give, we shall receive.

Ant Thinking. This alternative focuses on small thinking. Never a giant prayer or wish or longing. Just get me through till payday.

Lately, Americans have been fascinated with the word *excellence*. The 1984 Summer Olympics encouraged us to "go for the gold." However, the Olympic "moments of glory" followed years of agony, disappointment, frustration. The winners lived a winner's life-style a long time before they reached Los Angeles.

A life-style is what you are inside. How many of us drop the expected tidbits about our singlehood to lead others to conclude, "If only I were . . ."

Your life-style is as distinctive as your fingerprints. It's your choice. Don't let someone form it for you. Don't let the world squeeze you into its mold.

A life-style must be transparent, honest, authentic. That means we share the good, the bad, and the ugly!

Many single adults feel like imposters. They feel that if others knew them, really knew *them,* they wouldn't like them. So they hide. They divvy up their lives into stingy portions.

Life-style is always fluid, changing. Life-style is always a decision. Sometimes life-style involves struggle, a choice between options. That's why Paul warned, "Watch your life and doctrine closely" (I Tim. 4:16a, NIV). Simply stated, our life-style must not contradict our beliefs.

We have a tendency to select certain verses of scripture and ignore equally demanding sections. Thus, many singles would recite the old line, "I don't drink, gamble, or chew or go with guys/girls that do." What about our economic choices and our attitudes toward minorities and injustices?

Ant thinkers tend to blame others rather than take responsibility.

The growing single adult is free from the restraints of ark, ash, ape, ask, and ant thinking.*

ADMITTING INFERIORITY COMPLEXES

> *The Lord does not look at the things [singles look] at. [Single adults look] at the outward appearance, but the Lord looks at the heart (I Sam. 16:7a, NIV).*

If only my ___ were ___, then—

Perhaps you've heard the story of the single adult who went for months for counseling. Someone had told him that he had an inferiority complex. One day, his

---

*For more on this theme, see Harold Ivan Smith, *Positively Single* (Wheaton, Ill.: Victor Books, 1986), pp. 115-27.

psychologist said, "I have news for you. You don't have an inferiority complex."

"I don't!" the man exclaimed.

"No. You really are inferior!"

Millions of single adults struggle with low self-esteem. For example, because Bill missed an easy Ping-Pong shot, he put his hand through the game room wall of the apartment complex. Later, he explained to the manager, "I don't know why I did that. This feeling just came over me."

In fact, the feeling had begun earlier that morning. "This feeling" has been a frequent psychological parasite for Bill and for other singles. The feeling is low self-esteem. Whenever you entertain them, such accusations become entrenched house guests in the corridors of your mind. They prod you to prove your low self-esteem.

Some single adult leaders and psychologists believe inferiority complexes are the plague of the twentieth century. Too many single adults enthusiastically misinterpret Paul's words, "Do not think of yourself more highly than you ought" (Rom. 12:3, NIV), occasionally to ridiculous and scary extremes. Millions of single adults are handicapped not by rebellion or sin, but by a "who would want to go out with me!" (or worse) put-down.

Ironically, in some religious circles, low self-esteem has been praised as a virtue. Now it is big business. Advertisers stroke our inferiority feelings by suggesting that brand X product will make us feel "adequate" (or better). No wonder you don't have a date tonight. It's because you didn't use brand X.

Our roots of self-esteem are primed. You freeze if someone asks, "Do you smell something funny?" Sure enough you run through a mental checklist—mouthwash, toothpaste, cologne, deodorant—before you breathe again.

Think of all the things you splash on, spray on, smear on, spread on, swallow, gargle, and chew before you leave your apartment in the morning. Someday, a single adult is going to trigger a chemical chain reaction and disintegrate before the bathroom mirror.

Listen to this ad for one popular cologne:

Two powerful bands of fragrance energy. One for him. One for her. Each capable of triggering an intense magnetic reaction between the sexes.

____ cologne for man transmits powerful signals to any female within sensory range [how far is that?]. Its virile scent magnetically draws her to you.

____ cologne for woman silently sends enticing appeals to any man's subconscious. Its soft-spoken, yet powerful fragrance magnetically lures him to you.

These potent scent substances are, in fact, capable of stimulating the senses. To create a feeling of attraction.

For some, it's too risky not to use the products. "I need all the help I can get," one single man wailed.[2]

Ironically, many great people of faith have struggled with feelings of inferiority. Look over the following statements. Guess the identity of the biblical character.

1. _____ "Who am I, O Sovereign Lord, and what is my family, that you have brought me this far? . . . Is this your usual way of dealing with man?"

2. _____ "But I am a worm and not a man."

3. _____ "I am nothing but dust and ashes."

4. _____ "How can I save Israel? My clan is the weakest in Manasseh, and I am the least in my family."

5. _____ "O Lord, I have never been eloquent, neither in the past nor since you have spoken to your servant. I am slow of speech and tongue."

6. _____ "After me will come one who is more powerful than I, whose sandals I am not fit to carry."

7. _____ "Do you think it is a small matter to become the king's son-in-law? I'm only a poor man and little known."

8. _____ "I am a man of unclean lips, and I live among a people of unclean lips."

41

ANSWERS

8. Isaiah (Isa. 6:5b, NIV)
7. David (1 Sam. 18:23, NIV)
6. John the Baptist (Matt. 3:11b, NIV)
5. Moses (Exod. 4:10, NIV)
4. Gideon (Judg. 6:15, NIV)
3. Abraham (Gen. 18:27, NIV)
2. Psalmist (Ps. 22:6, NIV)
1. David (II Sam. 7:18-19, NIV)

Low self-esteem does not vanish at conversion, confirmation, baptism, graduation, *or marriage.*

But God can turn strength into weakness. Eleanor Chestnut, a missionary physician in China, said, "One thing that made me feel that I ought to go [to China] was the fact that there was no one to mind very much if I did."[3] God used her, in spite of her low self-esteem, to save hundreds, perhaps thousands, of lives.

Remember, God is no respecter of persons or physiques. Peter insisted that God "accepts [single adults] from every nation who fear him and do what is right" (Acts 10:35, NIV).

Single adults have to recognize and admit their inferiorities. Then, they can begin to dismantle them.

DIFFUSING INFERIORITY COMPLEXES

"Lord Jesus, receive my spirit" (Acts 7:59, NIV).

Denial only compounds the problem of inferiority!

O.K., you've admitted that you have an inferiority complex. That's a big step because some of your best friends would have a hard time believing you. Many times I have heard, "What would you feel inferior about?"

There are three big questions:

1. Can I do anything about it?
2. If I can, am I willing to pay the price?
3. If I can't, am I willing to change my attitude?

Take a minute and think about the thing(s) that make you feel inferior. Can you remember the first time you felt that way? Who encouraged you: a parent? a girl friend? a brother or sister? a teacher? Now, keep those questions in mind as you look at some of the barriers to diffusing your inferiority.

1. *Denial.* In counseling, single adults sometimes say, "Well, I have this friend who has this problem—" Some people deny low self-esteem because of the notion, "*If* you were where you ought to be spiritually, you wouldn't have this problem." A few think the inferiority will go away if it is ignored.

You can keep denying it and trying to cover it up but it is still there. You probably won't find help until you admit your need.

2. *Anger.* Bill, in the last chapter, vented his anger against a wall. Too many single adults vent their anger on other people. Paul asked, "Shall what is formed say to him who formed it, 'Why did you make me like this?' " (Rom. 9:20*b*, NIV). God wants to undo the consequences of our environment, not reinforce them.

3. *Negotiating.* Some single adults become victims of low self-esteem by trying to earn the acceptance of the significant others (parents/friends/teachers/dates). One way is saying, "I can't help it—this is me!" Another strategy is to work feverishly to eliminate a source of inferiority thinking, "Ah, *then* they will like/date/love me." How many single women have lost weight only to discover their dating life remained dismal? What then? They regain the weight, munching away their pain.

4. *Impatience.* We comprise the instant generation. We want it now or *now!* What do you do if the car in front of

you doesn't move instantly when the light changes to green? Do you honk if you love Jesus? Honk if you are horny? Honk to get that pile of junk out of your way?

Many single adults want instant answers or simplistic solutions. Many race to the nearest plastic surgeon or seize the latest diet craze. Many join health clubs but stop going after a few weeks.

By this stage in your life, the root causes of poor or low self-esteem are comfortably entrenched within your psyche. It may take the equivalent of Roto-Rooter to evict them. After all they have been nourished by a steady diet of reinforcement. It will take persistence and time to dismantle them.

In fact, some single adults struggle with second- or third-generation problems. The source of the inferiority (large nose, small breasts, hair texture, body type) is genetic.

What can a single adult do about low self-esteem?

1. *Face the problem.* Denial only makes the roots thicker. David prayed, "Renew a right spirit within me" (Ps. 51:10, KJV). We must not only acknowledge the problem to ourselves, but also to the Lord. You are encouraged to "cast your cares on the Lord" (Ps. 55:22*a*, NIV). It also helps to admit our need to others.

2. *Gather more data.* What stimulates poor self-image? If you have identified some/most of the roots, ask, "Why does *this* bother me?" Double-check original sources: your memory, conversations with parents or long-term friends.

Then read. We have a rich heritage of popular psychological materials and resources. Remember, there is no original inferiority. Other people have struggled with the same or similar problems. Sometimes you can conquer your inferiority through their help. Two books on this subject that I highly recommend are: *Healing for Damaged Emotions* by David A. Seamands and *One of a Kind* by M. Blaine Smith.[4]

3. *Tackle the negative feelings.* Poor self-image can be useful, can even be a convenient excuse. Poor self-image eliminates risk and solicits empathic strokes from some people. "You poor, poor dear!" Many single adults miss significant growth opportunities because of the residue from previous failures. Healthy psychological growth and maturity require risk.

4. *Consider the alternatives.* Ask yourself the following questions:

- How will I feel one, five, ten years from now, if I am still struggling with this? Poor self-image is an exhausting burden which destroys relationships and prevents us from forming new ones.
- Am I modeling a behavior that others will emulate? Self-image problems sometimes run in families, for children learn from their parents. You can break the cycle.
- How would I feel if I could go a whole day/week/month/year without this feeling sapping my energy?
- Am I willing to allocate the time and energy to dissolve the sources?
- Am I willing to seek professional help?

"A shrink?" Hey, you wouldn't self-treat yourself if you had a broken tooth or broken arm. What you have is a broken self-image. There are professionals trained to help you.

Everyone, *everyone* (including celebrities and pro athletes) deals with self-image problems. The arrogant, the conceited, even those with superiority complexes, are playacting. Dr. Paul Cunningham in a Mother's Day sermon, 1981, College Church of the Nazarene, Olathe, Kansas, expressed it well: "Just as God heals people physically through a skilled physician, so he heals people emotionally through a skilled counselor."

5. *Thank God for what you do have.* In our world, we are bombarded with incredible wants. We fail to be thankful for so many things we take for granted. Have you ever

thanked God that your feet are the same length, that you can tell the difference in colors, that you can hear and distinguish between thousands of sounds? Paul said, "Do not be anxious about anything, but in everything, by prayer and petition, *with thanksgiving,* present your requests to God" (Phil. 4:6, NIV, italics added).

During her singleness, Joni Erickson (Tada) overwhelmed me with a simple statement. To a group of single adults she said, "You think you have problems in dating. How would you like to be on a date and have to have your bladder bag changed?" She scored a direct hit with that question.

6. *Invite God to help you.* God is anxious that I become the person he dreamed I could become, the first time he thought of me. The psalmist wrote, "My frame was not hidden from you when I was made in the secret place. When I was woven together . . . your eyes saw my unformed body" (Ps. 139:15-16*a,* NIV).

Too many single adults are like children quipping, "I can do it myself!" Let God help.

CHASTITY

For the grace of God . . . teaches [singles] to say "No" to ungodliness and worldly passions (Titus 2:11-12, NIV).

There is nothing wrong with the word *no.*

Chastity is a word we don't hear a lot about today, although Sonny and Cher named their daughter, Chastity Bono. What is chastity? Webster says, "Abstension from sexual activity; said *especially of women*" (italics added). Even the dictionary bows to the pressure of the double standard. But in God's lexicon there is "neither Jew nor Greek, slave nor free, male nor female, for you are all one in Christ Jesus" (Gal. 3:28, NIV). Celibacy is for *both* genders.

Chastity is a synonym of no. The writer of Titus described the chaste person by noting that grace "teaches us to say 'No' [capitalized] to ungodliness and worldly passions, and to live self-controlled, upright [not up*tight*] and godly lives in this present age" (Titus 2:12, NIV). We don't need to flee to a monastery to avoid temptation, for it would follow us like a shadow.

Rosalie de Rosset explained chastity powerfully in an article in *Christianity Today*.

> I am 33, mentally and physically healthy, reasonably content, and single. Because I am single, I am also chaste by choice and conviction. I am not more given to sexual temptation than the average person, but neither am I less susceptible to it. I have the normal amount of sexual energy for a person of my age with the feelings that attend it.
>
> By chaste I mean chaste; I do not engage in sexual activity. Furthermore, I do not indulge in games too often played by singles wishing to relieve their boredom while remaining technically short of the line. I do not flirt with married men, have occasional flings with single men, or develop unhealthy attachments to other women. Not being an athlete, I am not prone to sublimation by means of hard exercise. As a lifetime member of Weight Watchers, I am scared to overeat. I overspend only occasionally. And I hate cold showers.
>
> I am not a saint. Then how do I do it? I have heard that question in the church for years from both marrieds and singles. . . .
>
> Clearly, if one is single and chaste, he/she must at least be fighting the demon of lust on an hourly basis. An occasional lapse reassures the inquisitive of one's normality; compassion and understanding abound for the fallen single.
>
> There is little praise for the consistently sexually controlled single. Too often, it is mixed with granulated pity of powdered condescension. Ironically, while discipline and self-control are encouraged and admired in scholarship, athletics, music, and ministry, their absence is strangely excused in sexual matters. The secular myth

has infiltrated the Christian consciousness: our sexual urges are overpowering and irresistible. There will come the moment when we "simply can't help ourselves," when "madness" will overtake us, when "it will be bigger than us." To resist the madness is somehow a failure to comprehend true sexuality, to be pronounced neuter—if not audibly, then certainly subconsciously.

How do chaste singles do it? Very simply (not easily), we keep our commitment to our convictions. . . .

Goals, hard work, solid friendships, and taking God at his word have played a part. Taking one day at a time, understanding our own natures, and knowing what to avoid all probably help. Believing that God has given us our singleness at the moment, that our condition is not an accident or a cosmic joke, also figures in. More obviously, perhaps we have learned that no one gets everything he wants. Everyone has an itch he can't scratch, regardless of position or circumstance.

But this is America on the edge of the twenty-first century, you argue. De Rosset concluded:

There will always be somebody to suggest that such thinking is legalistic, unreasonable, and unlikely to succeed. My reply can only be: "When it's bigger than I am, so is God."

PUNISHMENT

God is not mocked, for whatever a [single] sows, that he will also reap" (Gal. 6:7).

Sometimes even Jesus chose silence.

"You'll reap what you sow!"
"The wages of sin . . ."
"Serves you right!"

The writer of Psalms insisted, "We spend our years as a tale that is told" (Ps. 90:9*b*, KJV). Every speaker at a youth camp or teen retreat has had a repertoire of stories about "the consequences of sin."

Morality has traditionally been fueled by three fears:

- fear of infection
- fear of detection
- fear of conception

A generation ago, a lot of macho men carried condoms in their wallets, perhaps somewhat like a rabbit's foot. Most of them saw so little action that by the time they were used, they were defective. It was a sign of readiness, but also an acceptance, to a degree, by the man of responsibility for birth control.

However, with the onset of the pill, men transferred the responsibility to women. Hence, we're seeing a spiraling rise of venereal disease and related social diseases, even though many guys say they only did it with "good" girls. Yet, VD is no respecter of persons.

The fear of detection was obviously ignored if you were dating an insecure male, who in a moment of bragging in the locker room, let "the cat out of the bag." No wonder your phone became so busy!

But a missed period had a way of slowing the pulse and breath for a while. And how many women tearfully and sincerely promised God, "if you get me out of this, I'll—"

But there are aspects to punishment.

1. *God.* "God is not mocked, for whatever a [single] sows, that he will also reap" (Gal. 6:7) are stern words of foreboding. Many think of God as an accountant "keeping score" until one day he's had it with us. Wham! The divine zap.

God loves us and therefore must discipline us. The punishment may hurt, but it does not harm. We have so endowed God with human qualities, particularly a short fuse, that we forget the words of Samuel, "God does not take

49

away life; instead, he devises ways so that a banished person may not remain estranged from him" (II Sam. 14:14, NIV).

In Lamentations we read, "Because of the Lord's great love we are not consumed" (3:22, NIV). Yet, "men are not cast off by the Lord forever. Though he brings grief, he will show compassion, so great is his unfailing love. For he does not willingly bring affliction or grief to the children of men" (3:31-33, NIV).

Nor will God ignore or accommodate our standards.

2. Self. The body and mind may cooperate to produce consequences, which may often be pseudo. I had a friend who became convinced he had VD. Yet, the tests were negative. Instead of relief, he replied, "I have a kind they haven't discovered yet." When pressed, he continued, "I deserve it for what I've done."

Punishment can be self-fulfilling. And many single adults have revealed their own transgressions—or left a trail of evidence—in order to be punished.

3. Others. "I'd rather have God catch me," one of my single adult friends said, "than some Christians. God would be easier on me!"

Job's friends did not make his suffering any easier with their charges, "You know what's wrong with you, Job." Pseudo-friends invade our privacy to act out the role of prosecuting attorneys or amateur detectives.

Yet, the overlooked reality is found in Job 42:10, "*After* Job prayed for [those miserable] friends, the Lord made him prosperous again" (NIV, italics added).

4. No Punishment. Some remember those immortal words of a parent, "Just wait 'til your Father hears about *this*" (and the implications were negative). Others of us had brothers and sisters who blackmailed us with their threats to report x, y, or z to our parents. That sense of impending doom ruined many afternoons. So it is with life.

Sometimes, there are no consequences; after all, God looks at the heart of the guilty. And there were those times in our lives that we're glad are over.

The overenthusiastic storytellers often focused on "forever and forever" consequences to sexual choices. That could be true but sometimes it is linked to the person's need to be punished rather than to God's intent. We must remember that in the Old Testament many of the sexual sins had enormous penalties which did more to prevent the practice than to redeem the sinner.

When Jesus confronted the woman "caught in the act," he chose not to be punisher. He spoiled the party for those who had volunteered to be executioners.

In that moment, Jesus chose silence—stooping to write on the ground. The woman's accusers sneaked away. Perhaps, we would be better examples of his grace, if we were silent more often.

EASY

"Everything is permissible for me"—but not everything is beneficial (I Cor. 6:12a, NIV).

If there are macho men, there have to be easy women, because thinking women are seldom impressed with macho-linity.

Women have to say yes if males are to have the sexual experiences that underwrite the double standard and shore up fragile male egos. Unfortunately, the woman who "gives in" reinforces a guy's conclusion that he "has a way with women." Thus, he expects his charm to work on the next woman. As mentioned before, he doesn't believe a no means *no*.

Few women want to appear easy, but some have such an intense craving to be loved that sometimes it reaches a proportion that overwhelms reason. In others, it is a longing to be accepted by a certain social group. But any woman who gives herself away must be aware that men talk. The word is going to get around.

There are women who are teasers. They lead men on, then retreat. Intimacy becomes somewhat of a game of wits. Some single adults translate the liberty of grace into license (Gal. 5:13), although Paul warned against such a false assumption. Many women do not understand the signals they send. Men develop strategies to overcome the most subtle insecurities. Paul hinted of those who had "itching ears." What is true with doctrine is also true with sexual practice.

Men, particularly those who have been hurt, also send out signals. Hence, some women have become walking emergency rooms where men can recuperate. Once the men recover, they set out to form a new relationship. Some women have had a string of wounded individuals whom they have helped get back on their feet emotionally.

The single-again faces a related problem. Jesus warned of men who devoured widow's homes (Mark 12:40). Many want an asterisk to permit a sexuality for those who are single again.

So, some hint, "You're only a virgin once!" They reject any naiveté. Some crudely insist, you *need* it. Surprisingly divorcees are approached by married men (often friends) because of the crude cultural myth that once women are sexually initiated, they must be "serviced." Many friendships have been terminated or strained because of such a faulty assumption. This is one reason wives put distance between the new divorcee and their spouse. Women accept the myth as much as do the men. Thus, many divorcees and widows experience enormous pain—deserted by a mate, isolated by friends.

In reality, saying yes may be easier after divorce, particularly if anger is a strong motivator. If the ex-spouse is playing the field, it stimulates an "I'll show him" or "two can play that game." However, such a rationale always brings new scabs and fresh tears.

If you have been easy, the good news is that you do not have to continue to be so. There is freedom from the chains of the past in Jesus Christ.

SUBLIMATION

Be careful, however, that the exercise of your freedom does not become a stumbling block to the weak (I Cor. 8:9, NIV).

Cold water is seldom effective in dousing hot libidos.

Most Christian single adults have heard the verse, "Whatsoever things are pure . . . think on these things (Phil. 4:8, KJV) or Paul's injunction, to "avoid every kind of evil" (I Thess. 5:22, NIV). So, how can you live under the weight of "if God knows my thoughts, I'm a goner"?

Frequently, the Scripture cites self-control as a virtue (Gal. 5:22; Titus 2:12). Paul urges us to "purify ourselves *from everything* that contaminates body and spirit" (II Cor. 7:1, NIV, italics added).

"The grace of God . . . teaches us to say 'No' to ungodliness and worldly passions" (Titus 2:11-12, NIV). In sublimation, unacceptable impulses are transformed into socially acceptable actions. Freud contended, for example, that when society prohibited sexual expression in direct sexual means, alternatives had to be found. The positive and creative patterns are sublimative.

Athletics become a way of sublimating sexual energy. Now, in a day of permissiveness, some peers do not appreciate your sublimation. They reason, "Why not be sexually active?" Such people "think it strange that you do not plunge with them into the same flood of dissipation [i.e., debauchery, lust, drunkenness, orgies, carousing], and they heap abuse on you" (I Pet. 4:4, NIV).

Attitudes about self-control have had a lot to do with the notion that "idle hands are the devil's workshop" and that cold showers are a great remedy for temptation. I heard of a single adult who went to his pastor about his excessive sex drives. The pastor began praying loudly, "O God, help this man. Give him strength to resist."

The man interrupted, "But, Pastor, I've tried prayer."

Next the pastor suggested that cold showers would squelch hot libidos. "But, pastor," the man protested, "I can't pay my water bill anymore!"

Single adults must learn to channel their sexual drives in ways that will not offend. Thus, what one finds sublimating may be questionable to another. Many single adults find masturbation a subtle sublimation of the sex drives. It rechannels the drive from illicit sexual intercourse. Many singles regard masturbation as the lesser of two evils.

Paul encouraged, "Be careful, however, that the exercise of *your* freedom does not become a stumbling block to the weak" (I Cor. 8:9, NIV, italics added); we must guard against wounding the weak conscience. But, as with celibacy, sublimation must not become a source of pride.

Paul demanded, "Since you died with Christ to the basic principles of this world, why, as though you still belonged to it, do you submit to its rules: 'Do not handle! Do not taste! Do not touch!'?" (Col. 2:20-21, NIV). It was not only evangelicals who had high standards on sexual morality. Colossians noted, "These are all designed to perish with use, because they are based on human commands and teachings" (Col. 2:22, NIV).

There is the danger of pride in such teachings, "Such regulations indeed have an *appearance* of wisdom, with their self-imposed worship, their false humility and their harsh treatment of the body, but they lack any value in restraining sensual indulgence" (Col. 2:23, NIV, italics added).

God looks at the heart. God has given us the ability to avoid sin *through* his strength rather than ours, lest we should boast. "The Lord knows how to rescue godly men from trials" (II Pet. 2:9, NIV).

In a paraphrase of Psalm 119:9, "How can a single adult keep his way pure" (especially in today's sex-saturated society)? "I have hidden your word in my heart that I might not sin against you" (Ps. 119:11, NIV).

The comfort is that we will never be tempted above what we can endure and God will provide a means for you to cope with it (I Cor. 10:13). Often, that is sublimation—cutting the drive off at the pass.

REJECTION

Do not let any unwholesome talk come out of your mouths (Eph. 4:29, NIV).

Reject the relationship, not the person.

Two strong motivations influence the sexual behaviors of single adults: (1) rejection and (2) the fear of rejection. The latter can be as paralyzing as the former, because it is a logic based on presumption rather than reality.

It begins in adolescence when we choose and are chosen. Have you ever been the last one selected on a ball team? Or worse, have you sparked a debate: "You take him. No, *you* take *him*"?

We're all afraid of being rejected. This leads people to "grease the pan" or "set the stage" for their big moves. Some men plan the super date and spend a lot of money so that the woman feels obligated to accept future dates.

Other men have a sliding scale of sexual expectations based on how much money they spend.

One way to test the possibility of rejection is by joking or lightly suggesting something—to get the other person's response. This adds an ongoing tension as one tests the responses for implicit permission or the hint of rejection. Many people operate under the philosophy, "Nothing ventured, nothing gained."

However, because of women's liberation, more men are having to say no, and many feel threatened when the female becomes sexually aggressive or initiates intimacy. In such instances, a man may want to say no but is afraid the woman will think she doesn't turn him on or that he is gay (and according to research by Altman, 14 percent of single men are homosexuals[5]).

Individuals must be extremely careful to reject *the act* or the level of intimacy rather than the person. Certainly, some will challenge the no with more persuasion.

Some women tease, set men up for the wrong moves as a test of their attractiveness. Such action never excuses sexual impropriety.

And remember, we have a fundamental right as single adults to say no as a way of saying yes to what is best for us.

INTIMACY

"Mary . . . sat at the Lord's feet listening to what he said. But Martha was distracted by all the preparations that had to be made" (Luke 10:39-40a, NIV).

Single adults are more intimacy-starved than sexually deprived.

In a generation used to instant cereal, tea, or television, many single adults want instant intimacy. Many equate intercourse with intimacy. Yet, millions of singles have shared the sheets but never the soul. Tragically, despite many anniversaries, there are thousands of married couples who have never known intimacy.

I'm not sure I can define intimacy. It's a feeling, an emotion based on commitment. It is a lowering of the drawbridge so that you can cross the moat into another's soul. It is the man/woman inside the suit of armor.

Calderone and Johnson have suggested that the ultimate meaning of intimacy is that two people delight each other and delight in each other in an atmosphere of security based on mutuality, reciprocity, and total trust. Art Carey in *In Defense of Marriage* defined intimacy as:

- believing in someone and something above and beyond yourself
- developing a private vocabulary and communicating without words
- having someone who truly cares, someone who will stand by you when you get sick, or falter or fail
- having someone you believe in, and who believes in you, tell you at times that you're the best, and at other times, that you can be much better
- having a common history and mutual memories and the sense of having traveled together[6]

Intimacy creates a sense of "being dazzled by the private magnificence of another" person. However, before that can happen a trust level must have been developed that allows disclosure. Sidney Jourard said that when a person knows where to put the *balm* to heal me, he knows where to plant the *bomb* to destroy me.[7]

Consequently, many single adults live behind the walls, afraid of intimacy, yet desperately afraid that they will die without ever having genuinely known it. Intimacy may replace diamonds or gold as this society's most valued commodity. Its rarity ensures its value. It goes back to Adam and Eve "naked and yet not ashamed." Intimacy says, "I trust you with my vulnerability."

Intimacy requires time, so there can be no such thing as

instant intimacy. That is why the counterfeit sexuality of one-night stands and "I'll call you tomorrow" wound and maim. Many swinging singles have had eager lovers warm their beds but never their hearts. Intimacy requires more time than many singles are willing to invest. However, those who make a commitment receive handsome dividends.

Intimacy requires risk. Single adults come to new relationships generally to meet their needs after the failure of an old relationship. We scowl at the potential of any new relationship to meet our need. So, just in case, we limit our investment and thereby deny the fertile environment in which intimacy could develop.

Intimacy requires communication. We must reveal what we are seeking. While intercourse is expressed through the genitals, intimacy is generally expressed with the ears. When listening to a person, I allow him to be himself. Abraham Schmitt in his book *The Art of Listening with Love* (Abingdon Press, 1982) insists, "There is healing power in listening." Listening is the invitation for another to open that long-locked door to a secret corridor within the spirit. It is never a thoroughfare but a path, for few will ever be allowed to enter. Yet, in that quiet corridor we discover the potential of a person.

Thus, there are single adults "who have long been waiting, in the shadows, for someone to come along with a gentle hand, a tender heart, a sensitive soul, and open ears." When single adults *mutually* share their inner fears "they discover a kinship that they have not known before, and as a result, the transforming power of intimacy is unleashed."[8]

Genuine intimacy is proportional to the depth of a relationship. "You go deeper and deeper," says Carey, "into each other until there are no secrets left, no illusions, nothing but respect for each other's frailty and dignity."[9]

Few people, whether married or single, will ever achieve their dreams and potential without having tasted of genuine intimacy. Intimacy requires a long apprenticeship.

Terry Hershey in *Intimacy: Where Do I Go to Find Love?* (Nelson, 1987) reminds us that we are all "emotional orphans in search of a home." God has given us a capacity for intimacy; indeed, a hunger for intimacy so intense that no one can satisfy it. That reality led God to conclude, "it is not good for the man to be alone." That reality led Jesus to share himself with twelve disciples and to select from that twelve, three for a deeper relationship, and one, John, was the beloved disciple.

What an injustice has been done to single adults through the attempt to equate intimacy with intercourse. How tragic that so many unmarried adults have settled for endless orgasm-producing activity that is less lonely than masturbation and less involving than marriage.

Intimacy is a delicate gift.

LONELINESS

God sets the lonely in families (Ps. 68:6a, NIV).

Loneliness is a decision!

How do you spell loneliness: a-l-o-n-e? Does loneliness take up all your time alone?

Recently, throughout a manuscript I consistently misspelled loneliness, omitting the first "e." The editor quipped that a person suffering from a fatal disease ought to be able to spell it correctly if he is going to complain so much about it!

Single adults are armed with emotional "night-lites." We do not want to be alone in worship, at McDonald's for a snack, or in our sleep or old age. Where do all the lonely people come from?

Loneliness is one consequence of our prized value of privacy. "Just leave me alone!" demands the average single adult besieged with junk mail and numerous interruptions by telephone solicitors or salespersons. Single adults live behind security gates. Single adults have the option of ignoring the buzzer. Yet, the more one struggles to preserve privacy, the more the spirit complains of loneliness.

One study in New York discovered that thousands of single adults do not say one word from the time they leave work until they return the next morning. One service sells phone calls. Subscribers are called twice a week "just to chat" for a nominal monthly charge.

Many single adults form *isolationships*. Why get to know the neighbor across the patio or hall? The neighbor may move next week anyway.

I once thought single adults had a corner on the loneliness market. I too had read the scripture "it is not good for the [single] to be alone" (Gen. 2:18a, NIV). I concede some hours have more than sixty minutes; some days have more than twenty-four hours. However, recently, I discovered that loneliness is a common denominator for humans whatever the age, faith, sex, or marital status. We do not discard loneliness when we marry; we merely share loneliness creatively with another.

Too many expect marriage to end those feelings. Marriage cannot shore up sagging egos or personalities. We do not become complete through a mate.

Moments of aloneness are necessary to block out the din and roar of our sound-cluttered society. In this age of expected background music, where do we find silence? How do we get alone with our thoughts? Our stereos, televisions, cassette players, and radios become emotional baby-sitters or companions.

Silence threatens. "Someone say something!"

Loneliness may revolve around mealtime or bedtime. Many read or watch television until they fall asleep. Job spoke of wearisome nights full of tossing to and fro (Job 7:4). David reported his weariness in trying to fall asleep (Ps. 6:6). You may nod in agreement.

But aloneness can be an investment. A time to recharge our emotional/spiritual batteries. Aloneness can be a time to plant seeds. We can profit from aloneness by following the psalmist's direction, "When you are on your beds, search your hearts and be silent" (Ps. 4:4, NIV). Ironically, loneliness can be a fog to block us from the harbor of aloneness, where time alone can give the insight for the solution to a problem, or rest after a battle, or the grace to deal with a crisis.

Single adults need moments of aloneness: to reflect, to meditate, to hear, to think, and to re-create. Some priorities must first be tested in the quietness of the spirit. Some yeses must first be rehearsed in solitude. Some decisions can best be made beside a babbling brook or looking at a sunset. One single parent laughed and said she didn't have time to be lonely. Her few moments of aloneness were in the daily shower and even then—

Aloneness is necessary to block out the din and roar so that we may hear the cadence of the heart. Jesus could not have conducted his ministry without moments (hours and even days) of aloneness—nor could Moses, Abraham, or John the Baptist.

In *Warm Reflections,* I wrote:

I am alone!
I have accepted my aloneness.
I have not cursed it,
    nor have I welcomed it for a prolonged visit.
At this point I choose to be hospitable
    rather than face a duel.
Aloneness is an abstraction,
        a coloring-book word,
    and the coloration I choose to grant it
        will define whether I become
            a warden to aloneness or merely a prisoner.

My question is are you the *prisoner* or the *warden* of your loneliness. It's your choice.

DATING

"Get her for me. She's the right one for me!" (Judg. 14:3c, NIV).

Every date is one date closer to the big date!

Dating has been labeled the scourge of modern single adult living. Few single adults have positive affirmations for the process. "It goes with the territory," snarls one woman. After all, many singles do not want to date in the first place; they'd rather be married. Some are angry that they have to date. "It's like running for student council in junior high school. 'Hi! Vote for *me!*' "

Dating raises a lot of barriers. Here are the realities.

1. There's always someone dating more frequently than I am. That's reality although it would be nicer if they wouldn't spend so much time talking about it. No wonder they don't have time to come to Bible study anymore.

2. There's always someone I would like to be dating. Some of us don't have problems getting *a* date, but dating the person we want to date is a different story. Among many single adults there is a subtle notion that a bad date is better than no date. Therefore, it's O.K. to use a person until someone better comes along—a bit of a romantic baby-sitter, so to speak. And there are those who believe they can win a heart if only given a chance.

In the Old Testament, Samson's father tried to talk the Hulk Hogan-lookalike out of a certain "young Philistine woman." The father pleaded, "Isn't there an acceptable woman among your relatives or among all our people?" (Judg. 14:3a, NIV).

But what is "acceptable"? Obviously, father and son had different criteria.

A son asked his father to borrow a lantern.

"I didn't need a lantern when I courted!" the father snarled.

"Yes, and look what you got!" the son replied.

I had a friend whose favorite post-date words were "you can do a lot better than that."

A residue remains from adolescent dating—if I go out with a *somebody* then I'm not a *nobody!* We spend a lot of time ingeniously scheming to get someone to go out with us. That's the reality that keeps so many situation comedies on television.

3. Every date is one date closer to the *big* date. Some single adults date with an agenda. They only go out with people they would marry. So, they pre-sort date, eliminating any risks. Tragically, they rely too much on first impressions.

The American commitment to falling in love rather than growing into love sabotages many relationships. In essence, it becomes an abortion of the emotions. Fantasy plays a significant part in our relationship formation.

How have the following influenced your expectation of a date:

- movies
- teen dating
- fairy tales
- romance novels
- songs
- youth camps/teen groups

Fantasy, although a hush-hush word among many Christians, is still a reality. We have a reasonable sketch of Prince/Princess Charming. Webster defined fantasy as "the power, process, or result of creating mental images modified by need, wish, or desire."

Single adults start gathering resource material for

fantasies early in life. Actually, it's like collecting materials for a term paper: a little from here, a little from there. Talk to kindergartners. Many already have notions, particularly physical attributes. As they grow older, they will add to and subtract from the stockpile.

Television and movies have been a major source in most of our lives. Women long for an Eric Estrada, John Ritter, Tom Selleck, Richard Gere. Yet, the likelihood of meeting even a close facsimile is questionable. Besides, there is tight competition.

Dating can be part of that captivating influence that Paul warned us to avoid. Some single adults' emotional life and self-image are correlated with their dating.

Somehow it's easy to wait for dates that fit our agenda. How heroic to mumble, "I'm saving myself." Men are just as unreasonable. Men dream of a woman as intelligent as Jane Pauley, as charming as Cher, as physical as Bo Derek, as musical as Anne Murray, with the coyness of Meryl Streep. And if she is all that and only twenty-five, think what she'll be like at fifty!

There is a tendency to incorporate celebrities, whether Christian or secular, into our dreams and expectations. So like Samson, we demand, "Get *her* for me. She's the right one for me." He said this before he had even met her.

But fantasy resembles idolatry. Some of us, by this juncture in our lives, have so nourished our fantasies, that no human could fulfill them. No wonder we're alone. Similar thinking got the Israelites into trouble when they attempted to fashion their concept of God into a golden calf. How many of us have pictures of Mr./Miss Right hanging on the walls of our minds? How many say, "No one else need apply."

It's great to sing, "Some enchanted evening, you may see a stranger, across a crowded Bible study/K Mart/and somehow you'll know." Yet, a popular gospel chorus, "Jesus Be the Lord of All" has a phrase about "the kingdoms of my heart." It is in the heart kingdoms that our expectations are stored and carefully stroked, particularly on lonely nights when we do not have dates.

Because we all have fantasies, we suspect that we fall short of another's dreams. Consequently, we look only at the shell rather than at the basic substances of the person.

Paradoxically, some have finally gotten a date with *the one*. They have had the sweaty palms, giggles, palpitating heart and have discovered the date was tuned to one station: **WME** or **WMYSELF**. The big date is a disappointment.

But what is a single adult to do? How will you ever escape singlehood if you don't date?

We'll look at that next.

SURVIVING DATING

> *See to it that no one takes you captive through hollow and deceptive philosophy, which depends on human tradition and the basic principles of this world (Col. 2:8, NIV).*

Some dates aren't worth it!

I have a single friend who opens every conversation with one question, "How's your dating life?" The previous conversation could have focused on the Middle East, nuclear energy, or the team that is going to win the pennant, but Dave's focus is the same—dating. He's an economist and explains, "It's the best trend indicator of your singleness."

Many single adults consider the subject taboo. Occasionally, when I am grilled about my dating, particularly by married adults who've watched too many episodes of "Three's Company," I have a routine answer. "I can understand why you would be curious about my personal life. But I hope you'll understand why I am reluctant to talk about it."

But some of us know more about the dates in a grocery store than we do about what many think is the chief benefit of the single life.

Here are some hints.

1. *The old rules don't apply.* It used to be "boy dates girl." Now it can be man dates man/woman dates woman/or gay dates straight or any of the above tag-team for a night on the town.

Perhaps we need dating referees with striped shirts to keep the dating fair. Dating is especially confusing for those who are newly single (it's O.K. to be bewildered!). Some professional football teams had difficulty when new rules, designed to increase scoring and excitement, were implemented. Just as rules change in the National Football League, so do the rules in dating.

Today women *do* ask men out. Some men say yes; some say no. Whichever, it's reality in today's world.

2. *A lot of people aren't dating.* It's safe to take reports about dating and divide by two or four. It's easy on a Friday or Saturday night to self-flog if you don't have a date. Are you *really* the only person in the entire world without a date?

When I lived in a trendy adult complex in San Diego, I discovered the pool area was abandoned on Saturday night. The apartments circled the pool, and if the residents looked out their windows at 9:30 P.M. and saw someone swimming, it was obvious that person did not have a date. Some residents had too fragile an ego to risk that conclusion.

3. *Some dates aren't worth it.* Many single adults, especially the desperate, put themselves into dating situations and then pray for deliverance. There are weirdos, crazies, and loonies out there in Dateland. Some people will subject you to an in-depth monologue on their life; your task is to

listen. Some single adults think that x expenditure of funds automatically entitles them to y amount of intimacy. And some have problems with the word *no*.

Doorway wrestling is just as repulsive as the mud variety.

4. *Finances are important.* The myth that the man pays and the woman enjoys may be true in adolescent dating. But in today's liberated world, if you insist on that standard—I hope you like reruns—you're going to stay home a lot. Of the 64 million single adults, 46 percent were previously married. For many after child support, alimony, and rent they do not have a lot of warm or cold cash for dating.

Women who reach for the check or who do not feel threatened by going international ("Dutch") date more often.

5. *When/then thinking is unproductive.* Some single adults think:

"When I lose twenty-five pounds, *then* I'll date."

"When I get a new job, *then* I'll date."

"When I attend a particular single adult group, *then* I'll date."

This makes dateless evenings easier to handle because the person decides, "It's really my fault that I don't have a date."

Suppose you lose the weight; that's no guarantee you'll date.

6. *Possessive dating is discount relationships.* A lot of dating is a flea market for bartering fringe benefits. Some singles become so attached to these benefits that they cannot terminate unwholesome relationships.

Some men want women who can cook or sew or clean or type. Some women have difficulty not using guys for home maintenance, automobile repair, and security. One of my friends, a CPA, is never lonely during income tax season. Harry, a genius auto mechanic, has a host of women friends who won't date him because he has grease under his fingernails, but they keep his phone number handy for those times when their cars won't start.

7. *There are a lot of walking wounded in Dateland.* The battle scars for some single adults are evident. Be with them five minutes and you've got the unabridged story of their life. Ironically, it's not only the divorced/widowed who have war stories. Some never-marrieds can easily top them.

One friend observed, "I am weary of playing mop-up nursemaid to recently 'dumped' guys. I'm tired of being an emergency room for the emotionally wounded."

8. *Some just want to "be friends."* Suppose I am clinging to the fantasy of Prince/Princess Charming. I need something to tide me over until the tardy prince/princess arrives. Just as a snack may solve cravings for nourishment until the big meal, so some individuals use relational snacks or mini-relationships to tide them over. They invest enough to keep the door ajar but not enough to be inclusive. They won't commit themselves long enough to see if there is a potential for a permanent relationship. They need to be footloose and fancy free. Besides, something better may come along and it would be difficult to dump someone gracefully.

Tragically, in the snacks, sometimes someone may think: *if* I keep giving and giving, *eventually* he/she will fall in love with me.

Quite frankly, many single adults do not want to risk. That's why some single adults (and others!) keep their money in passbook savings accounts rather than in a money market with higher interest.

A lot of single adults have pals, special friends, or buddies. This is one of the luxuries of singlehood. If they were married, some of their relationships would threaten their mate. But there are people who listen, share hot coffee, and say, "Call me if I can help."

Christians need to remember one thing: their dating life is not the indicator of their wholeness. Christians need to be cautious with such phrases as "I care," or "I love," which can be misunderstood. Christians need to be alert to the danger of "snowballing" relationships based on desperation.

BREAKING UP IS SO HARD TO DO!

Speaking the truth in love, we will in all things grow up (Eph. 4:15, NIV).

Making up is a lot easier than breaking up.

It is said that breaking up is very hard to do, particularly toward the end of the summer. Many single adults have discovered that making up is easier than breaking up. How do you terminate a relationship with class?

The problem is even more complicated in single adult groups. What happens when a couple who has met in the singles group decides to break up? Too many times both leave the group. While single adult groups do not exist to encourage dating per se, inevitably people meet and date. Sometimes their awareness of each other and their common commitment to the group give them a lot to talk about.

Some single adults take dating too seriously. Therefore, candidates must be pursued and excused before Mr./Miss Right comes down the pike. Some single adults go from group to group doing aerial reconnaissance.

But suppose you've given the relationship a chance. How do you end a dating relationship without sabotaging the friendship or acquaintanceship?

1. *Put-Downs: You.* The first response of many single adults is to blame the other person. "You are too _____." If we convince ourselves all the fault for the failure was

the other person's, we may feel more comfortable exiting. We also gain appreciative sympathy from others.

2. *Put-Downs: Me.* Many single adults have a low self-esteem. In their minds the mumble, "I don't deserve someone as nice as you" or "I'm no good for you." A few single saints are long-suffering and seem to attract the losers or those with poor self-image.

3. *"I'm not ready for this yet."* Often this statement is preceded by a "now, don't take this personally, but—" Many single adults ask one destructive question, "Is this the best I can do?" Perhaps you remember Groucho Marx's classic self put-down, "I wouldn't want to belong to a club that would have *me* as a member!"

Many single adults who nourish that fantasy of the perfect single adult are reluctant to make any commitment. However, this response is supposed to be less threatening, because it does not totally negate the worth of the ditched party.

4. *The incident.* Many people get restless in a relationship and begin looking for fire escapes or u-turns. So something happens: a faux pas, an irrational or insensitive response, and immediately the relationship is over. (It helps to make "over" very melodramatic.) This is especially evident in relationships where communication has been poor or when the incident triggers memories of previous breakups. Sometimes the offending party never understands why the incident was so significant.

5. *The habit.* If the person is looking for a rationale for an exodus, another escape may be "the habit." Lateness, insensitivity, hygiene, or racial attitudes are seized as a justification. Some divorcees are so oversensitized to a particular habit of a former spouse that the absence of that trait or behavior in their date causes them to overlook other equally frustrating habits.

What are some guidelines for constructively ending a dating relationship?

1. **Do not use one another.** Some relationships are an equation: X does this and I respond in a manner to keep the scales balanced.

2. **Do not prolong an inadequate relationship.** It's normal to have difficulty pulling the plug. The tears, the hurts, the accusations, the anger, the loneliness produce anxiety. But too many relationships have been prolonged by the mechanics and the fringes which are not unlike a dying patient whose life is prolonged by a machine.

There is a tendency to prolong relationships around birthdays or holidays. Many make payments on a gift months after the relationship has ended.

3. **Communicate.** Some single adults are genuinely surprised to discover the inadequacy of the relationship. "Why didn't you tell me that you felt this way?"

A frequent answer is, "I didn't know how to tell you." Some singles are so afraid of hurting or of creating conflict that they retreat rather than make disclosures that could strengthen a fragile relationship or terminate an unhealthy one.

4. **Avoid accusations, digs, slashes.** The person is naturally hurt by the termination and does not need the excess weight of sarcasm, anger, or a tongue-lashing. "Oh, yeah, well what about the time I—" Such responses do little to affirm either partner.

5. **Don't manipulate.** Some couples "cut the other down to size" every so often. Kiss and make up can be a lot of fun. Others use the fake exodus to elicit a profession of love. If a couple avoids dealing with the realities of the relationship, they have not grown.

Finally, there is an ego-commitment that stimulates some to be the first to bail out rather than being a victim.

Ending a relationship is not easier for the Christian, but a Christian's commitment to doing the right thing will give some guidance and support even when the lights go out.

APPROACHES —————4

SINGLENESS AS AN OPPORTUNITY

An unmarried man is concerned about the Lord's affairs—how he can please the Lord (I Cor. 7:32b, NIV).

You don't become a spiritual giant by saying "I do"!

How do you view your singleness? A problem? A mystery? An opportunity? We've heard a great deal about "the hand that rocks the cradle, rules the world." That had ties in our historical roots. A colony needed people. D'Emilico wrote in *Sexual Politics, Sexual Communities* (University of Chicago Press, 1983) "the imperative to procreate" dominated colonial thinking.

However, by the late 1740s, Conrad Beissel organized a commune that attracted many single adults. He sang, "And even if I find myself alone on my pilgrim's way, God will provide for me all along many a comfort and a blessing."[1]

Numerous American movers and shakers did not find their singleness a handicap. They chose to emphasize their *adulthood* rather than their single status.

- *Florence Nightingale* revolutionized nursing
- *the Grimké sisters* fought slavery through their tracts and speeches
- *Catherine Lee Green* financially supported Eli Whitney's work on the cotton gin
- *Carrie Catt* lobbied successfully for the nineteenth amendment, the right of women to vote
- *Phillips Brooks,* Episcopal minister, wrote "O Little Town of Bethlehem"
- *Luther Rice,* a founder of the Baptist denominations, was a missionary strategist
- *Francis Asbury,* first bishop of the American Methodist Church; his bachelor circuit riders organized hundreds of churches
- *David Brainerd* was a missionary to the Indians
- *Hans Christian Andersen* wrote delightful fairy tales that have charmed millions of children
- *Annie Jump Cannon,* Harvard professor and astronomer, named 250,000 stars
- *Susan Elizabeth Blow* opened the first public kindergarten in America

These people etched their names in American history. Yet, there are thousands more *in pectore* or in the heart of God.

I think of Sylvia Dickinson, who carried the news of the fall of the Alamo to General Sam Houston.

I think of Emily Perkins Bissell whose Christmas seals helped reduce the commonness of tuberculosis.

I think of Liz Bailey who brought joy to thousands of children through her circus.

I think of Martha Berry who opened a Sunday school for poor mountain children in Georgia which later became Berry College.

I think of Dag Hammarskjöld who as Secretary General of the United Nations died working for peace in the strife-torn Congo.

I think of Donaldina Cameron who rescued hundreds of teenage girls from San Francisco houses of prostitution.

I think of Sophia Palmer who lobbied for state registration and higher standards for the nursing profession.

I think of Rachel Carson whose book on DDT alerted this nation to the dangerous side effects of chemicals on our environment.

I think of Katherine Lee Bates who wrote "America the Beautiful."

I think of May Craig who was the first woman to fly over the North Pole and challenged reluctant guests on "Meet the Press."

I think of Dorothy Hansine Anderson who discovered cystic fibrosis.

I think of Dr. Virginia Apgar who was the financial genius behind the March of Dimes.

I think of hosts of unnamed single women who dared brave the prairies to tame the West through public schools.

I think of hundreds of women who defied social standards and entered nursing during the Civil War.

I think of sixty-year-old widow Mary Bickerdyke who braved Southern bullets and the wrath of northern generals to hold boys on both sides as they bled to death. She dared to look in the eye of one general who demanded, "On whose authority are you here?" She responded, "On the authority of the Lord God of Israel and unless you have higher authority than that, leave me alone!"

I think of those hundreds of brave women who traveled to the far corners of the earth in the wave of missions after the Civil War. They challenged emperors and social customs such as foot-binding. They shattered ignorance and tackled poverty.

These single adults did not see themselves as "half-persons" because they were not married. They were too busy teaching school, founding colleges, staffing hospitals, training nurses, challenging the powers-that-be. As a result the world hasn't been the same.

Many were teased, harassed, questioned, even imprisoned, yet they saw singleness as an opportunity. Maybe some of them thought, as do many contemporary single adults, "I could *better* serve the Lord *if* I were married—if I were part of a dynamic duo!"

These single adults did not become spiritual giants or movers and shakers by saying, "I do," but by saying, "I will by the grace of God be what he wants me to be!" They seized the opportunity where others saw only disappointment.

But I often wonder, as great as these people were, who will take their place? Who will dream the great dreams of the last of the twentieth century? Who will dare to risk, to challenge?

I keep rereading the words of Mordecai to Esther, "And who knows but that you have come to royal position for such a time as this?" (Esther 4:14*b*, NIV).

That is my question to you. "Who knows but that _____ (fill in your name) has come to royal position for such a time as this?"

Would you be willing to see your singleness—of whatever duration—as an *opportunity?*

SINGLENESS AS A PROBLEM TO BE SOLVED

> *Do not be anxious about anything, but in everything, by prayer and petition, with thanksgiving, present your requests to God (Phil. 4:6, NIV).*

Too many single adults see singleness as a problem to be solved.

The question, Why aren't you married? sounds like a simple one. Yet, you may offer a flippant or surface answer and be unaware of the real answer to that question.

Some people see life as a problem. If only x, y, z, or whatever were different, then my difficulties would be solved or eliminated. How shallow the taste of victory must seem to the one who discovers a few weeks into a marriage that nothing has changed.

Indeed, the person I am as a single adult is who I will be married. Saying "I do" does not change a person.

In fact, singles who see singleness as a problem set themselves up for disappointment. They see a mate as an answer, not a person. Some singles enter marriage with an ulterior motive: the fathering of a child. Some women want someone to love them. An adult seems a bit of a challenge, so they decide to have a child. However, because of the social stigma they do not want to have a child out of wedlock, so they deliberately choose a potential mate who cannot make them happy. Then after a year or so of marriage and a successful pregnancy, they have what they wanted. The stigma of a divorce is a small price to pay for the acquisition of someone to love—a child.

There are three consequences to perceiving singleness as a problem to be solved.

1. *It paralyzes your potential.* If you perceive singleness as a season to grow, to stretch, you can have experiences that will enable you to become all that you can be. However, the person who sees singleness as a problem is tempted to take the first possible solution or exit. Many single-agains are persons who have chosen divorce as a way of uncovering their potential that they abandoned at the time of marriage.

2. *It ruins your relationships.* Because every date merits the question, Is this the one? the single adult has few friendships. The art of getting to know people is enhanced through singleness. To say, "I'd never go out with a man or woman I wouldn't marry," only heightens the frustration of datelessness. Soon one is tempted to

lower or alter the standards. The scent of desperation has frightened off many potential mates.

3. *It sabotages your Christian service.* It's hard to be a Kingdom-seeker when your mind is on your naked wedding finger. Christian service is more than an alternative to datelessness or a way to fill space on an empty social calendar.

When people see singleness as an opportunity, they often immerse themselves in activities and mission. Sometimes they meet others through involvement in a single adult ministry. Through "project intimacy" or working on a project together they have a chance to get to know someone better than they had known them before. A relationship develops.

Many couples have met in a single adult group. It's not that the group was a place to meet someone. Rather, when giving themselves, they released an element of attraction. This is not unlike the Old Testament story of Ruth who met Boaz as a result of working the grain harvest. Boaz first recognized Ruth's work, then her charm.

Problems are meant to be solved. Yet, impatience leads to solutions that become problems themselves.

SINGLENESS AS A CONSEQUENCE

And Tamar lived in her brother Absalom's house, a desolate woman" (II Sam. 13:20d, NIV).

It's not so much what happens to me as how *I choose* to respond!

"You can't cry over spilled milk!" is a common cliché in American society. "Let bygones be bygones" is another. In fact, a common theme in situational comedies has been the reappearance of a former fiancé the star *might* have (or should have) married.

Tamar, the beautiful daughter of David, was raped by her brother, Amnon. Because of the Jewish preoccupation with virginity, Tamar was now used and therefore "unmarriageable." The Jews didn't know about the ovum; they thought that semen was life itself. The Jews didn't know that sperm died. Thus, they thought, if a woman had had sex five years earlier that sperm *might* be still in her womb. So to protect a husband's ego from the fear that another male might be the father of his heir, virginity was essential.

It didn't matter that when a woman lost her virginity, either by choice or consequence, she also lost her and-they-all-lived-happily-ever-after ending.

Tragically, that still happens. Tamar lived her life "a desolate woman," no doubt well-provided for, and her dreams remained nightmares. Every royal marriage only reminded her of what she had lost or missed out on.

Your singleness may be a consequence of a broken engagement; worse, your singlehood may have been a consequence of divorce. Worse yet your fiancé or ex may have married someone else, and now that door is shut, nailed tight. Newspapers relish stories of couples who have finally gotten together, twenty, thirty, forty years after they had originally parted.

The gospel teaches us that we are not mere victims of the bad things that happen to us. Rather, we can convert any tragedy, any defeat, into victory.

I think of Catharine Beecher whose fiancé died in a shipwreck. In those days, it was considered honorable never to marry if one's fiancé died. Catharine didn't mope, "Oh, poor me." Rather she became involved in the westward migration. She developed a set of principles which later became home economics. She committed herself to improving homemaking. She also added guidance counseling (in a primitive manner) to public education. She recruited hundreds of women to go west to become "school marms."

Thus, in conquering her tragedy, she helped tame the West.

Now, will you decide to conquer your tragedies?

It is not so much what happens to you as how you *choose* to respond.

Some singles are choosing to modify the classic "poor me/old maid" syndrome. Many are outrightly rejecting it. The society in which we live offers abundant opportunities to those who refuse to be (or remain) victims. Much of the blatant discrimination in housing, employment, credit that taunted single adults a decade ago has been removed.

"If onlys" and "I should haves" keep people linked to the past rather than drawn to their futures. "If onlys" lead many to jump/leap to the *next* relationship. "Rescue me," they croon. Some grit, "I'm not going to let *this one* get away."

I think of Sally Johnson, unmarried, who went to the missionary field. She rejected the stereotype of an old maid. She exercised, watched her diet, read, took risks. After forty years, she retired without family or significant savings, yet she had a lifetime of rich memories. At the retirement complex in California she met a widower. Well, someone had to show her the "ropes"—where the bank and post office were. In the process of time, they fell in love and married. Sally called it "God's big surprise" for a lifetime of obedient service.

Another missionary, Dorothy Blatter Ross, also married after she retired.

Then there was Mary Regier Hiebert, who didn't marry until she was seventy-seven.

Possibility thinkers "never say *never*." Don't ever totally count out the possibility. Recently I heard about a ninety-three-year-old man who married—his first trip to the altar. He said, "All these years I've heard so much about marriage. Just thought I'd try it!"

Too many Tamars of today overromanticize those old relationships. "It would have worked if only—"

Maybe it would have worked, but maybe not.

But what about today? Are you ruining a perfectly good today rehashing yesterday or romantic leftovers?

Or are you currently involved in a dead-end relationship because Prince/Princess Charming got away. Or are you a widow troubled by the taunts, "If only I had gotten him to go to the doctor." As a divorced person, you have far clearer vision today. You know the things you should/could have done. So admit that and proceed. Today shouldn't go to waste.

As a jogger, I have to pay attention or I'll get lost. One day in Hattiesburg, Mississippi, toward the end of the run I saw a shortcut and took it. About a half mile later I discovered I was on the right road back to the motel. If I had taken the other road, which I had assumed to be longer, I would have been going in the wrong direction. Because of left-rights, I had ended up on the right path.

Some of our lives do take left turns, right turns; even u-turns. God directs us.

I concede that the consequences can be painful. But *you* can be a survivor. Use this season of singleness (however long or inconvenient) to make a difference.

SINGLENESS AS A MYSTERY

This is a profound mystery—but I am talking about Christ and the church (Eph. 5:32, NIV).

The mystery leads to either misery or mastery.

"If only I knew why no one wanted to marry me, *then* maybe I could do something about it."

Sometimes curiosity gets the best of people, and the question finally slips past their teeth, "And just why are you single?" In some instances, the question is embellished, "What's a sweet young thing like you doing unmarried? If I were single, I'd snap you up in a minute!" And they actually expect an answer to the question.

There is a mystery about singleness. It's a mystery to me why some folks are married, get married, or stay married. At times I wonder why some single adults are unmarried: they have so much to offer.

Americans have a tendency to be overly analytical. We scrutinize everything from our soil to our election results. Put it under a microscope. Dissect it. But sometimes, after the introspection, we're still no closer to an explanation than at the beginning. A valid explanation evades us. Simply, the best and most accurate response may be, "Beats me!"

Would it make a difference if you knew why you were single? If you *knew* that, would you ever marry?

One reason young single adults are generally threatened by older single adults is the menacing fear that it could happen to me! I could end up old and alone. It's one thing to be young and single but it is another to be old and unmarried.

I remember one friend of mine continually asking, "Why can't I get pregnant?" A string of obstetricians had not been able to answer the question. After she and her husband adopted a child, the question became moot. A year after the adoption, she was pregnant.

There comes a time to put aside the philosophical to embrace the mystery. My friend is married to a minister. Often, in her pain, she prodded him, "If God helps other women get pregnant, why doesn't he answer my prayers?"

Her husband's "I don't know" only enraged her.

"You're a minister. You're supposed to know."

"Well, you may have to wait and ask the Lord yourself."

We cannot live our lives on hold. Some women have not been overly enthused with the singles movement. One admitted, "I've been too busy using my rights to debate my rights."

Our task as single adults is to trust God to lead us through this season. To give us confidence to fully experience the mystery.

SINGLENESS AS A CHOICE

> *But each [single] has [her] own gift from God; one has this gift, another has that (I Cor. 7:7b, NIV).*

A noted family authority interviewed Luci Swindoll, author of *Wide My World, Narrow My Bed* (Multnomah Press, 1982). "When did you decide to become single?" he asked.

This authority had previously interviewed Carolyn Koons, author of *Tony: Our Journey Together* (Harper & Row, 1984), also a never-married career woman, who had responded, "Oh, I didn't decide. I'm just not married. I haven't ruled out marriage."

However, Luci is not Carolyn.

"When I was seven," Luci replied calmly.

"Huh?" the interviewer asked, surprised that a seven-year-old could make such a decision.

Many young never-marrieds resist the classification "single." However, a few have realized that they will probably be single the rest of their lives. They choose to respond to that rather than react. Dorothy Payne explained:

For me, the turnaround came when I began understanding that to be single and thirty-eight was not the end of life but could be a fresh beginning. I came to realize through loving friends that there is a God who cares and loves, a Spirit who calls us to new life and supports us in our search for different values and the inner power that is ours. I came to know that single women have to unlearn old patterns that no longer work for them, and replace those patterns with new attitudes and responses. Thus we move toward being women who realize their potential for newness, freedom, strength, and joy.[2]

Moreover, "being single, with the responsibility of life squarely on our shoulders, can be a position of strength if we will accept it. Looked at this way, singleness is an achievement to take advantage of, not a condition to escape from."[3]

"Singleness is an [opportunity] to take advantage of, not a condition to escape." Yes, for many single adults singleness is a choice. At least someone's choice (a mate/a fiancée/a parent or men in general or women in general).

For some there is that growing awareness that "no one is going to marry *me*." Laurence Alma Tademan wrote:

> If no one ever marries me,—
>   And I don't see why they should,
> For nurse says I'm not pretty,
>   And I'm seldom very good—
>
> If no one ever marries me
>   I shan't mind very much;
> I shall buy a squirrel in a cage,
>   And a little rabbit-hutch:
>
> I shall have a cottage near a wood,
>   And a pony all my own,
> And a little lamb quite clean and tame,
>   That I can take to town:
>
> And when I'm getting really old,—
>   At twenty-eight or nine,—
> I shall buy a little orphan-girl
>   And bring her up as mine.[4]

I recently found a newspaper ad that read:

When I grow up
a rich man will
fall in love with me
and marry me
and take care of me.

The copy line added, "At Girls Clubs, girls learn that fantasies don't come true except in fairy tales." That ad reflects a new awareness of singleness. It's hard to believe that about seventy-five years ago, the President of the United States could take time out of his busy schedule to denounce singleness. In an address to the First International Congress on the Welfare of the Child, March, 1908, Theodore Roosevelt declared: "The greatest privilege and greatest duty . . . is to be happily married, and no other form of success or service, for either man or woman, can be wisely accepted as a substitute or alternative."

No sooner had he spoken than the *New York Times* challenged him. What about the contributions of such single adults as Jane Addams of Chicago's Hull House? Had he not praised her "as an example for all other women to follow"? Teddy modified his remarks. At that time the majority of Americans believed that each person had a *duty* to marry, to preserve the fabric of society, and to rear sons and daughters "for the sustenance of the Republic." This was particularly true of Protestants who were concerned about the Catholic birth rate and immigration.

Today, some would ask, "Why would someone choose not to marry?" As Americans become more comfortable with wholeness, fewer will struggle with choosing.

Certainly, a number of single adults have chosen to emphasize a career, *at this point.* Men especially reason, "I can always get married." Historically, the British chose single men to come to the colonies to work because they could get more work out of them. Some single adults have such a preoccupation with getting ahead that they have little or no time for romance. They give their best to IBM or ITT or Elmo Swartz and Sons.

There are also Momma's boys and Daddy's girls too tied to the apron strings. There are some men/women in love with themselves, leaving little room for anyone else. Some are homosexual. Twenty years ago, homosexual men or women married to hide their sexual preference. Some attempted to use marriage as a laboratory to convert to heterosexuality. Now, with the gay rights movement, they have more freedom not to marry.

Some people are in love with their dreams. Andrew Carnegie, for example, did not marry until he was almost fifty years old and extremely wealthy.

Finally, the current status of marriage has led many single adults to view it skeptically. Because some marry young, many single adults have high school or college friends who are already single again. A tremendous number of marriages last only a year or two. One mother complained to her daughter's landlord. "They're going to get a divorce and I'm still making payments on the wedding."

Too many single adults have been motivated by the whisper, "Don't let *this one* get away" and the ticking of the biological time clock.

Most single adults do not make a lifetime choice. The choice comes in increments, in seasons. Joseph, foster father of Jesus, illustrated this point. God told him to marry and to go to Bethlehem. Joseph obeyed. Then, in the middle of the night, God ordered him to take Mary and the baby to Egypt.

Why didn't God spell out the entire road map for

Joseph before he asked for a commitment? Simply, God disclosed and Joseph obeyed, a step at a time.

Julie Anderson said, "Fulfillment does not depend on our marital status—but on God's action in our lives."[5]

On January 4, 1960, Lillian reviewed her fifty years of humanitarian service in Egypt:

> On this day my heart goes back 50 years to 1910. I was a young, happy girl of not quite 23, full of dreams of all the wonderful things I was sure life held for me. The most important of all was the 12 children I was hoping for. I wonder what I would have felt like had the curtain been lifted for just a few minutes and I could have seen myself this morning, 50 years later.
>
> Here I am—a tired, old gray-headed woman, looking out my window and not seeing 12 children but 1,200! I believe the shock would have been more than I could have stood. *God, in His wisdom, softly draws the curtain of His love across the future of our lives and lets us live day by day* (italics added).[6]

Luci Swindoll agrees with such a commitment.

> I've had a wonderful life. If I were to die today, I would have few regrets, really. Even with the pain and heartache I've experienced, my life is filled with tremendous memories which I build upon constantly. I'll carry these memories into my old age. . . . We're often so concerned about the future; but when it comes, it's . . . you know, it's today. So: live today! That's my philosophy.[7]

I am also reminded of Elisabeth Kübler-Ross' statement, "To the extent we become captive of stereotypes, we limit all that we can be!"[8]

You may not have chosen singleness, but you can choose to be happy in this season of your life. Singlehood beats the other two alternatives: being dead or being married to the wrong person. One realist quipped, "It is better to go through life wanting what you do not have, than having what you do not want!"

ALTERNATIVES————5

DISCOUNT RELATIONSHIPS

This is my prayer . . . that you may be able to discern what is best (Phil. 1:9-10, NIV).

God never takes his kids to discount stores.

"No! You take them!"

It is not fun to be the last person chosen for a team or a group. That's the same way some single adults feel about life. That's what leads some single adults to accept "discount" relationships: 40 percent off. "Why pay more? Bargains galore at Discount City."

"Discount City" may well have bargains. But you have to decide if it's a bargain or not. And do you *really* need a bargain? "No one sells it lower," they advertise. "It's always on sale at Discount City!"

Some single adults are desperate for marriage. Some single adults have vast deficiencies of love, affection, and attention. Combine those feelings in one person and you will have trouble, perhaps causing the emotional equivalent of lightning on a hot summer night.

Desperate people rarely make good choices. That's one reason that rebound relationships are so dangerous. Let's face it; some people will settle for second (or third) place. They'll "make do."

Sometimes, when I fly I say to my travel agent, "Get me the cheapest fare possible. I'll even bring my own seat and parachute." Give me a Coke, magazine, and some peanuts and I will survive. But there's more to flying than that. There's first class. What a difference!

If God wants you married, he wants it first class. If God wants you single, he wants your singleness to be first class.

In too many lives there comes that intersection— almost the last chance. In that panicked moment, many have traded in first-class tickets for coach class life-styles. God has no discount life-styles. Jesus said, "I came that [single adults] may have life, and have it abundantly" (John 10:10).

Single adults are supposed to marry *up*, never down. But spiritually and emotionally, they often settle for less. Some Friday night, some Sunday morning, some Christmas Eve—when loneliness is at floodtide—they conclude, "Well, a bad marriage is better than no marriage!" Others couch it in progressive thought, "He'll/she'll change."

In fact, in an age of high divorce rates, we've modified the cliché, "Better to have loved and lost than never to have loved at all." Slightly paraphrased that reads, "Better to have been married [and divorced] than never to have married at all!" A strong, at-least-you-were-married attitude exists, particularly among single women. How often the burden falls on a single woman to explain why she has not married.

You must come to terms with your singlehood. Anger, resentment, pity bias your ability to think clearly. I call them p.t.r.s: prime time relationships. Most occur between Thanksgiving and Valentine's Day, when four holidays emphasize family and marriage and love relationships. I mean it's no fun picking out your own Valentine or heart-shaped box of candy.

On Sunday before Thanksgiving, I was sitting with a pastor and his family in a nice restaurant. I had enjoyed entertaining his two small children as we waited for our meal. As we ate we talked about the family's plan for Thanksgiving.

The pastor said to me, "Harold Ivan, singleness may be O.K. *now,* but what about thirty years from now?"

"What do you mean?" I asked.

"Don't you want a Benji of your own who would bring over his son to see good ole Grandpa Smith on Thanksgiving? Tell me you don't want that."

Well, I didn't have a good answer. Holidays are a type of Bunsen burner which increases the heat under our aloneness. Certainly, that day, the pastor scored a direct hit on my emotions (although I camouflaged well).

However, on Thanksgiving, I realized that not everyone—married or single—has a T-day worthy of the cover of *Saturday Evening Post.* There are a lot of couples whose "over-the-turkey" conversation is limited to such phrases as: "How's your turkey?" "Pass the cranberries." Or who rely on others to keep some type of conversation going.

Yet there are more non-holidays than holidays. And the loneliest person in *your* zip code will not be a single adult, but a married adult, lying on her side of the bed, thinking, "O God, when will it ever get better?"

There are a lot of things worse than being single, even on Thanksgiving.

No wonder Paul could say, "This is my prayer . . . that you may be able to discern what is *best*" (Phil. 1:9-10, NIV, italics added).

You will never have clear judgment if you're regularly attending "pity parties," even if they are black tie and catered. Still, singleness *could be* an apprenticeship to lead you into a mature adulthood, whether married or single. Don't settle for a discount relationship. You deserve better.

PERPETUAL ADOLESCENCE

In everything set them an example by doing what is good. In your teaching show integrity, seriousness and soundness of speech (Titus 2:7-8a, NIV).

Act like a child and they will probably treat you like a child.

"When are you going to settle down and get married?" That's a common question asked by parents, grandmothers, and aunts. One friend responds to such questions, "No man deserves as much love as I could give."

Some single adults think a dumb question deserves a dumb answer or a shocking answer. In one church foyer a man came up to a single adult and said, "Bill, I just can't understand why you aren't married." The single adult had just attended an assertiveness seminar and decided to try out his technique.

"I'm gay," he said, softly.

The questioner looked stunned. Slowly, he backed away, shaking his head. Bill had to work hard to convince him he was only joking.

But many parents and even psychologists think marriage is one of the essentials of successful young adulthood. In fact, Robert J. Havinghurst listed eight development tasks for young adults:

1. Selecting a mate
2. Learning to live with a mate
3. Starting a family
4. Rearing children
5. Managing a home
6. Getting started in an occupation
7. Taking on civic responsibility
8. Finding a congenial social group[1]

Because I found this list in a book published in 1958 I assumed that Havinghurst had restructured his theory in light of the growth of singleness. Surprisingly, in 1984, it was the same agenda. Oddly, for many of us, two or more of the first four do not apply. Are we therefore to assume we are immature?

Admittedly, for some, singleness is an extended adolescence. In America, in the last few years, there has been an increasing tendency for young adults to postpone their first marriage.

Between 1970 and 1978, the median age of persons marrying the first time increased one full year; since 1978, it has increased *another* full year. In 1983, the median for men was 25.4 years; 22.8 for women. The Census Bureau has concluded,

> This postponement of first marriage may be associated with a growing desire and tendency among young adults to pursue advanced education and labor force careers prior to marriage and may ultimately result in more persons never married.[2]

Many young single adults (particularly the "yuppies") are saying, "I'm not ready/willing to assume the responsibility of marriage." Some even add an exclamation mark. Barbara Ehrenreich discussed the evolution of the macho man (she argues men are the loudest in their unwillingness) into the "New Man" in her book, *The Hearts of Men: American Dreams and the Flight from Commitment* (Doubleday, 1983). She praised the males for their newly found domestic independence—they can fix their own quiche—but she lamented the fact that so many prefer to eat it alone. Indeed, bachelorhood, freed of its gay stigma, has become the male's territory. Perhaps there is some safety in numbers, for the "number of men living alone rose from 3.5 million at the beginning of the Seventies to 6.8 by the end." Most of these men have never been married, and 70 percent report that they find marriage (a la commitment) restrictive. One woman fumed because a man she dated was so frightened by commitment that he "checked out the fire exits in a restaurant before we sat down." Yet, the other side is the tragic number of daily divorce cases in which the couple married too young or because their hormones were at flood tide.

Some married adults decide the grass is greener and embrace singlehood as Adolescence II. Some nurse a lingering question (particularly in light of the alleged sexual freedom of single adults), What am I missing? For others it is a biphasic adolescence, an emotional maturation that did not accompany their biological sequence.

Several years ago I directed a national single adult conference for a conservative denomination. A few days before the conference, a concerned pastor called me, "What are you going to do with the chaperons during the day?"

"Chaperons?" I asked.

"Yes."

"We're not having any."

"What?" the voice growled. "You mean you're taking singles into a hotel without supervision. No curfews or room checks?"

"Pastor, some of these singles are fifty years old and quite capable of looking after themselves."

"Well, you won't get any single adults from my church!"

Well, they missed a great conference. Unfortunately, many pastors see single adulthood as an extended adolescence, this time without pimples. They have even programmed that logic into the local church. I would contend in an era of high divorce rates, the reluctance to marry is positive rather than negative.

The advice in Titus, "In everything set them an example by doing what is good" is sound. Single adults have more resources, more time to "do good" and "be good." Sometimes, that means resisting peer pressure and evangelical materialism. Sometimes it results in isolation.

Second, single adults are also reminded to show integrity, seriousness, and soundness of speech. The Bible states, "Watch your life and doctrine closely" (I Tim. 4:16*a*, NIV). Many single adults have their doctrine pat, but the life-style is another matter.

Tony Campolo contends that single adults have the best cars, jobs, life-styles, clothes, houses, and that leads to a concealed envy by some marrieds. Yet, it will take awhile for Americans to become comfortable with singleness—to learn it is a natural part of the life cycle of adulthood. Only when singlehood is accepted and "marital desperation" is diminished will the divorce rate decline.

Admittedly, singleness is a period fraught with dangers and confusion; a culture that will pay any price for youthfulness leads to some ridiculous extremes.

Single adults must challenge the stereotypes, misconceptions, and prejudice.

Sooner or later the realities have to be confronted. You are an adult and you have the right to resist any attempts to make you anything less. But you have an equal opportunity to lift the impression of singleness by leading an exemplary life, by making a commitment to be a Kingdom-seeker rather than "the swinging single" so common in twentieth-century folklore.

ATTITUDES————6

THE GRIPPERS

Who can find a virtuous [single]? (Prov. 31:10a, KJV).

There are few Mr./Miss Perfects out there, but a lot of Mr./Miss Rights!

Jim Towns in *One Is Not a Lonely Number* (Crescendo, 1977) has identified three classifications of single adults:

- grippers
- grabbers
- growers

Grippers are the people who give singleness a bad name. They are the malcontents who have sworn to be in a permanent state of frustration, anxiety, or boredom. Grippers dislike being single. They reason that life begins *when* they get married. Tragically, some are "single for a reason"—their bitterness at being single.

Grippers are stuck on two lines: "Where are the men?" or "Where are the women?" and "All the good ones are married!"

Most grippers have a list of qualifications for their potential mates that no human could possibly meet.

Grippers paraphrase the scripture to "who can find a virtuous single?" Grippers sit around waiting for

Prince/Princess Charming to show up on a white charger and whisk them away through the sunset into the land of ohhhs and ahs of alleged marital bliss.

A friend of mine recently moved from a beautiful apartment on a quiet street in a nice neighborhood. I was surprised and asked why.

"Oh," she laughed. "I was too far off the interstate exit ramp. Prince Charming has been getting off at the right ramp all along, but he can't find me in my cul-de-sac. So, now I'm right off the ramp. Any day, I'll be out there working in my flowers and he'll see me and—"

I softly hummed a verse of "Dream On, Dreamer, Dream On."

Grippers keep life "on hold" until they marry. Most have a grandmother/aunt/friend who whispers, "You know you're not getting any younger." Or an uncle who asks, "When are you going to settle down and get married?" More family gatherings are spoiled with such great questions!

Grippers view singleness as a prison sentence to be served—with time off for good behavior. A seventy-year-old woman responded, after a seminar, "But I'm tired of being good. I want a man." Conviction surged through her voice!

But grippers seldom realize that they are sending out a hardly disguised signal: *desperate!!!* which translates "Dangerous waters ahead. Proceed at your own risk."

Grippers are seldom dated. Thus, they may become jealous of friends who are dating. They may take a holier-than-thou attitude: "Well, I guess I could have dates too if I—" in essence, lowered my standards.

Because of the negative preoccupation, grippers cannot develop friendships with members of the opposite sex. Ironically, many single adults first develop friendships with those they eventually marry.

Worse, grippers always have a hidden agenda in attending any event: to scout the men/women. Single-again grippers use a stock line: "Isn't that just like a man/woman!" They are suspicious. They examine every social invitation for the fingerprints of matchmaking. "Why I'd rather sit home and burp my Tupperware than—"

Sometimes, out of frustration and acute loneliness, grippers give in sexually. Some have become grippers because of a string of sexual scars. Further dating only irritates the scar tissue.

Grippers live out self-fulfilling prophecies. They set themselves up for more temptation than they can handle. Grippers risk more hurt by dating neurotic, insecure people. Grippers may be angry at everything and everybody—including God.

Too many grippers think a bad relationship is better than no relationship. "So, I'd better hang on to this one *until* something better comes along."

Grippers sell themselves and other singles short. Often the very relationship they crave gets cut off at the pass by their negative life-style and philosophy.

But grippers can change. With a lot of affirmation and sometimes, confrontation, they let go of their old scripts. Sometimes a friend has to say, "You're gripping again!"

Perhaps you are a gripper. You don't have to remain in that mode. There's a better way of living, relating, and growing.

THE GRABBERS

If the Lord delights in a [single's] way, he makes his steps firm (Ps. 37:23, NIV).

A grab bag is only worth what you pay for it!

A single man called a woman and asked, "Will you marry me?"

Immediately she responded, "Sure I will! Who is this?" The grabber. Grabbers insist, "You only go around once. You've got to reach for the gusto!" Grabbers become impatient waiting for the Lord to provide a mate. They're ready to escalate the selection process. Instead of contentedly riding in the back seat, the grabber climbs over the seat and mumbles, "I'll drive!"

Grabbers date with a frenzy. Grabbers save time by pre-sorting potential candidates. They eliminate the Momma's boys, the Daddy's girls, the weak, the insecure, the broke. The older the grabber, the tighter the grasp. For many women grabbers the increasing loud ticking of the biological clock fuels the frenzy, and children are the *real* agenda. They say, "If the marriage doesn't work out, at least I'll have children."

Most single adults have had a season of grabbing. I heard one day about a man who got married. When the pastor read the vow to get his expected "I do," the groom looked at the bride, shrugged, and mumbled, "She'll do!"

Something similar happens at Christmastime. You're tired of shopping. Suddenly, Old Spice will do! (Besides he can always return it.) Some merchants anticipate the 4:30 Christmas Eve shopper's panic. Marriage panic is almost identical.

A lot of things stimulate grabbing.

Graduating fuels the senior shuffle (or scuffle) in some colleges, particularly in the church colleges that promote themselves as "a great place to meet a mate." One counselor quipped, "If marriages are made in heaven, this campus must be a branch office." Yet, a steadily increasing divorce rate is a consequence of spring semester grabbing.

The birth of a niece or nephew can cause the grabbing tendency. What do you do if you are the oldest sibling? "If all my brothers and sisters can find someone to love, why can't I?"

The death of a parent can prompt the emotionally

dependent or financially insecure single adult to marry quickly.

Seasons are influential. Christmas turns up the heat on some relationships. What a great time to announce an engagement! Valentine's Day is a great time to give a diamond.

The wedding of a roommate or close friend stimulates grabbing. For some women, stepping over a roommate's stack of copies of *Modern Bride* only complicates the stress.

Some people use sex to whet the appetite or bait the proposal. Even in a day of liberation it's still common. Others see marriage as a way to diffuse their guilt.

Promotions can enter into the picture. My friend John realizes that the conservative law firm for which he works will never make him a partner *until* he marries. The firm has a reputation to preserve. Already he's been bypassed by two persons hired after he was. Many companies still see marriage as bona fide proof of maturity and stability.

Some parents want grandchildren and have built a system whereby each of their children has to earn the parents' affection. This leads many live-ins to marry; to please a parent (or a grandparent who may have a generous will).

In a few families, trusts become functional at marriage. In fact, in such situations, many men married young to get their money.

Tragically, grabbers, despite their desire for marriage, rarely make good partners. Desperation is seldom disguised; its scent frightens off many good candidates.

Even worse are the people who discover, once married, that they married a grabber. Somehow the thick fog of romance clears and there is stark reality. No wonder people sing "Ah, sweet mystery of life, I found you!"

There's nothing wrong with wanting to marry and nothing wrong with having an incredible longing for a family. But if you allow the healthy to become unholy, arguing the means justify the ends, you're asking for a second season of singleness via divorce. In fact, your engagement may be the first step toward a divorce court.

I think that if you dare to abandon your desperation, you may have taken the first step toward marriage. You may have significantly improved your potential. Sure, people whisper, "Don't let *this one* get away," but all of us have missed a "bargain" and later felt relieved.

Grab bags have always intrigued me. There's something about a pile of bags and a sign: "Up to $7.95 in value. Your choice—only 99 cents." Well, if it's *really* worth $7.95 why sell it for 99 cents?

Grabbing is a choice.

THE GROWERS

"For I know the plans I have for you, . . . *plans to prosper you and not to harm you, plans to give you hope and a future" (Jer. 29:11, NIV).*

Even if I never meet you, I am going to be happy with the me I will live with until I meet you.

Growers are single adults who have decided, "I do not know how long I am going to be single, but I want to make the most of *this* season!"

Growers emphasize their adulthood rather than their singleness. Growers are adults who happen to be unmarried.

The psalmist wrote of that single who is "like a tree . . . which yields its fruit *in season* and whose leaf does not wither. Whatever he does prospers" (Ps. 1:3, NIV, italics added). Season, huh?

Suppose singleness is the season of winter.

I cannot tell you how long winter will last, but I do know that spring follows winter. Growers may have *gripped* and *grabbed*. But growers have come to appreciate the need for a single season—if only to work on the *me* they bring to marriage.

A friend owned a nursery and raised beautiful flowers for hanging baskets. I discovered that he used certain chemicals to speed up the growth cycle of his plants. At that time I was into petunias and asked if I could have some of the magic potion.

"Sure," he said, "but follow the directions carefully."

Well, I reasoned that if one drop would cause such massive growth, what would ten drops do? So I peppered my plants. You can imagine my stunned surprise when I found dead plants. I tampered with the season and killed them.

Growers have learned, even painfully, that there are worse things than being single. Growers are committed to stretching, exploring, becoming all that God invites them to be. They understand the wisdom of Ecclesiastes,

> There is a time for everything,
> and a season for every activity under heaven. . . .
> a time to weep and a time to laugh,
> a time to mourn and a time to dance, . . .
> a time to be silent and a time to speak. (3:1, 4, 7*b*, NIV)
> and
> a time to marry *and a time to be single.*

Some single adults get caught up with their list of characteristics for a desired mate, but growers wisely invest their time and energy working on the *me* they will bring to marriage or invest in other relationships.

Growers have decided that *even* if they *never* meet their mate they will be happy with themselves.

Growers have learned that God does not offer instant solutions.

Growers know that God's will for all his children is wholeness and the abundant life.

SELF-SEEKING

"Be on your guard against all kinds of greed; a [single's] life does not consist in the abundance of his possessions" (Luke 12:15, NIV).

Happiness is not a collection of trinkets.

"Now, maybe she'll go out with me" says the young man as he proudly and confidently displays his new hundred-dollar sweater.

"Bill," interrupts his friend, "it's your breath."

"My breath?"

Sure enough, after thirty seconds of propaganda, we return to the final frames to see a happy couple walking into the sunset. Love and mouthwash triumph again.

In reality, ten cents of mouthwash solved the problem, but he can't afford to ask her out because he spent his money on the sweater.

Many single adults assume their social life (perhaps even their marital status) would be changed if they somehow could change. Others decide to take a time-out from relationships and concentrate on accumulating trinkets. American society offers endless varieties:

- personal computers
- cars

- condos
- electronic gadgets
- stereos

If a mate doesn't arrive, at least you will have enough "toys" to keep you comfy for a while. Remember the cliché, the only difference between the men and the boys is the price of their toys. I recently saw this bumper sticker: "The one with the most toys, wins!"

Sometimes toys can lead to complications when or if you marry. Some hobbies, for example, become obsessions. Naturally, your definition of excessive differs from mine. Sara learned that toys or loot doesn't lead to emotional stability or maturity. She bit her tongue and thought, "He'll change *after* we marry." However, she discovered during the engagement that her fiancé's hobby attention span varied. He had a pattern of starting a hobby, growing bored, then abandoning that hobby for another.

Others are so hamstrung by financing the trinkets and accompanying life-style that they cannot be generous in ministry. Tom makes $26,000 a year but could not afford to attend his group's last retreat. That seemed unreal until I examined his finances. I found that he spends $1,800 a year on lunches and almost $550 on donuts and coffee.

"It's my money," he argues. That's true, but it keeps him from a lot of good things.

Other single adults struggle with *mallitis.* They're watching the evening news, chomping down the T.V. dinner, wishing the dessert portion were larger. Bam! It hits. They grab the car keys and the checkbook and dash to the nearest mall.

They're not sure what they are looking for, but somewhere in that mall is something they need. A fix, of sorts.

Admittedly, it is a great feeling to feel the gravitational tug on your fingertips as you carry several bags back to your car.

If it's a cash transaction, it may not be so bad, but often it is a credit transaction. Some single adults think their task is to wear off the plastic numbers on their charge cards. With the best of intentions they resolve to pay off the bill next month, but they make next month the next month, and so on, and so on. Some single adults shop when they are depressed or when they don't have a date. The mail the first of the month only brings a bill and another round of depression and possibly another round of buying.

Credit cards were hard to get in the past, especially for the divorced. Now, you're almost branded "unAmerican" if you don't have a wallet full of plastic. Try renting a car without a credit card. While on campus at the University of Southern Mississippi, I was stunned to discover the movement to grant undergrads their own credit cards rather than use Mom and Dad's. Thus, you have a line of credit to purchase your trinkets, to finance your life-style at 18-20-22 percent interest. More leads to more; bigger leads to bigger; better to better. It was best summed up in a t-shirt I saw recently, "I owe, I owe . . . so off to work I go."

A lot of single adults wish they could get out of debt but lack the will power to wean themselves from their cards.

I admit the trinkets can be nice. Jesus said, "A single adult's life does not consist in the abundance of his or her possessions" (Luke 12:15, my translation). He insisted that we be on guard against all kinds of greed.

Greed is fueled by coveting. According to Exodus 20:17, you shall not covet your neighbor's condo or car or ski equipment or vacation or cruise or anything that belongs to your neighbor. That sounds like vacation Bible school. Moses took the last phrase of the verse as importantly as the first.

The ads, commercials, the "wait till you see my new _____. You're gonna die!" stir up our object-lust. "The new improved" is a magic code phrase like "open sesame" on your checkbook. Forget about layaway. Take it with you. Drive it home. Instant gratification. Why deprive yourself?

Greed pushes us one step beyond necessity. For example, maybe it was simpler when stereo cassettes were $5.98.

I hasten to add that I am not against buying. I have my blind spot: books. But I am questioning indiscriminate or impulse buying. Few people die by waiting for it to go on sale—whatever *it* is.

When I married, I didn't have enough money to buy the diamond, so, I dressed up, went to my bank, and waited to see the branch manager.

"Why haven't you saved for this?" the banker asked.

"I have, but I'm short and Valentine's Day is coming."

"How will you pay it back?"

"Well, I'm a graduate student and work part-time," the conversation continued. He loaned me the money—a mere $250.

Today, I am my own banker. I have $1,000 credit limits on my credit cards. I'm not bragging. It's outrageous. Multiply that by the number of cards and unless I am disciplined, I am in big trouble.

I cannot allow my self-image and self-esteem to be shaped by my trinkets. Or by what I drive, own, wear, collect, accumulate. Trinket collecting keeps me from giving to ministry, particularly missions. It keeps me from such things as cruises or trips to Europe. "Oh, I can't afford it" this year with my current credit debts, but with denial and savings, I could enjoy a Caribbean cruise next winter. Some little nos here and there could make it possible.

Trinket collecting keeps me from building savings and making investments. Recently I gave away about $1,000 worth of books I thought I had needed. If that money had been put in a money market . . .

Even though I am a professional writer, I often check out new books at the library rather than buy them. That way, if after reading a hundred pages, I decide a book isn't any good, what have I lost?

You may be tired of renting an apartment but are convinced you can never accumulate enough money for a down payment on a house or condo. Perhaps not if you are currently trinket collecting. Many single adults continue to rent because they can't say no.

Some single adults who would like to be in business for themselves work for someone else because they can't say no and save enough money for a nest egg to start their own company.

Trinkets can keep you from the best life-style.

KINGDOM-SEEKING

Delight yourself in the Lord and he will give you the desires of your heart (Ps. 37:4, NIV).

I have a nightmare of having avoided all of God's opportunities for a Cinderella dream that never came true!

On my refrigerator is a yellow index card with the above sentence on it. I copied that from an article in *Faith at Work* and for seven years I have read and reread the card. Maybe you too have discovered refrigerators are a great place to put reminders (perhaps *inside* them too).

That card is a reminder of the commercial in which a man smacks his forehead and mumbles, "I could have had a V-8!"

Regrets are too common in the lives of single adults.

- I wish I had—
- I should have—
- If only I had—
- If I had it all to do over again, I'd—

Cindy felt called to be a medical missionary. That shaped her thinking in her third year of college. Then she discovered that pre-med majors don't date their lab partners (particularly if they are smarter). So Cindy changed to science ed, hoping to attract a man, but when she graduated, she still did not have a husband.

"Not to worry," her advisers encouraged her. "Prince Charming will show up in grad school." But he didn't.

Next Cindy taught high school biology for five years, still waiting. Gradually, she realized that she might wait forever for the tardy prince. As the saying points out, "To get a prince you have to kiss a lot of frogs." Cindy, like many single women, had grown weary of kissing frogs.

So, she started a nest egg, paid off her debt, and enrolled in med school. Today she's a doctor in Africa—still unmarried but fulfilled.

What a career and impact! She could have "had it all"—a Porsche, a condo, a stock portfolio, a great private practice. Instead, on a typical day, she puts in fourteen to sixteen hours in primitive medical conditions: touching, healing, saving lives.

Cindy's a Kingdom-seeker.

After her first furlough, she had no regrets. When she visited colleagues and friends in the States, she discovered they were longing "for something more."

What keeps you from being a Kingdom-seeker, a risker?

I think of Dr. Eleanor Chestnut, who survived on oatmeal in med school. When she graduated, she went to China. There she found a man who would not heal after an amputation. Eleanor did a skin graft from her own leg and without the benefit of anesthesia. Yes, the man healed. Grateful. Sure. However, Dr. Chestnut died in a riot trying to protect her clinic. Her dying act was to tear her skirt to make a bandage to wrap around the head of a small boy, also wounded in the rioting.

It's not only in medicine that Kingdom-seekers work. Many single adults are making their zip code area a better place by teaching school, by doing social work, by volunteering.

I think of Becky, working for a shoe-string-budget private agency, buying things out of her meager salary when the budget won't provide them, pledging too much at the annual pledge dinner, and spending hours with pregnant young girls.

I think of Jim, working on the campus of a private college, living out his faith in the classroom as well as in the student union.

I think of Karla, working for slightly above minimum wage in a nursing home, loving someone's mother, father, aunt.

I think of Beth, teaching in an impoverished Mississippi school district, giving 99.9 percent of her heart to her pupils.

I think of Dr. Mac, a skilled scholar who has spent her life in a church-related college, making $10,000 less per year than she could at a nearby state university.

I think of Steve, driving a clunker so that he can support two college roommates in Youth for Christ and Campus Crusade.

Fools! do-gooders! idealists! in the eyes of "swinging singles," but in God's view, Kingdom-seekers.

They have coached dreams and repaired wounded egos, they have counseled the troubled, the cowardly. They have sacrificed to wet-nurse another's dreams. I've seen their cars, noticed their shoes, but I've never been offended by their generosity.

Have we overpraised foreign missions and overlooked those missionary spirits in our own neighborhoods?

A Kingdom-seeker doesn't always do the sensational, the miraculous, the unbelievable. Kingdom-seekers are often not recognized and praised. Kingdom-seekers have chosen to say no to first-person-singular living, as well as hedonism, to give of themselves in portions they never could share if married.

It is in Kingdom-seeking seasons that God allows those experiences to reshape our attitudes, challenge our priorities, revamp our goals, and renew our spirits. A season of Kingdom-seeking can do wonders to shape a single adult into a more attractive person and thus more marry-able.

A season of Kingdom-seeking is not unlike the process in which a jeweler takes a raw diamond and shapes it into a stunning jewel. The potential was there all the time; it only needed liberation.

"Delight yourself in the Lord." How alien those words sound in our world!

A single parent had two boys; their grandmother lived with them to look after them when their father was on business trips. The father had always brought the boys a gift when he returned, but on one of the trips he forgot. The pattern had been that every Saturday morning the boys would come into his bedroom, jump up on the bed, and say, "What did you bring us, Daddy?" Then he would point to his suitcase.

This particular morning the boys didn't believe his "I forgot." Crestfallen they checked the suitcase. "How could you have forgotten?" they said.

"I'm sorry, boys, but I'll tell you what. After breakfast the three of us will go shopping and you can pick out anything you want."

That morning his boys didn't want cereal or cartoons. "When are we going shopping?" they demanded, every five minutes.

When they arrived at the store, the boys raced to the candy counter. "Get us a big bag of this, Daddy."

"Are you sure?" he asked and walked ahead.

In the clothing section, the boys wanted shirts.

In the toy section, they were sure they wanted games. Each time the father walked on. Then they came to the bicycles.

"Get us bicycles, Daddy!" they pleaded.

"But you guys said you wanted candy, then shirts, then games."

"No, Daddy. *This* is what we want! Get us bicycles." The father walked on but didn't hear his boys following. He looked back and saw that they were still on the bikes, giggling with delight.

Obviously, he could have bought them candy or shirts or games, but he gave the best.

Give Kingdom-seeking a chance.

ATTITUDE-SHAPERS—8

YOU

He who chases fantasies lacks judgment (Prov. 12:11b, NIV).

Be good to yourself.

You are one individual.
You are one single adult: male or female.
You are a whole individual.
You have choices to make.
You decide to be obedient or disobedient.
You cannot assume responsibility for what others do.
You are a sexual being, with God-given drives and needs.
You can experience joy and peace and contentment.
You have the right to say yes or no.
You inherit consequences for either choice.
You can become the person God dreamed you to be the
   first time he thought of you.
You either conform to the world's standards or are
   transformed by his.
You are not the lone ranger.
You can choose not to feel inferior.
You can choose not to be lonely.
You can choose not to judge other single adults.
You can choose to honor integrity.
You can be a whole person in Christ!
You are not weird but are very special.

And because of these realities, you can make a
difference!

YOUR PEERS

He has made everything beautiful in its time (Eccles. 3:11a, NIV).

It used to be a common song: "Wedding bells are breaking up that old gang of mine." The singer was already feeling lonesome.

Our peer relationships are crucial shapers of our attitude toward singleness.

"Never! Never again!" snapped a single woman. "No more roommates, ever!" She stomped her feet dramatically to illustrate her determination.

"Why?" I casually asked.

"Because they keep getting married on me. It's not that Prince Charming can't find my apartment. My roommate always gets to the door first."

Someone summarized the feeling with a simple phrase, "Always a bridesmaid, never a bride." One woman, a bridesmaid one too many times, refuses to go to wedding rehearsals. "I've got the routine down pat," she huffs. Unfortunately, in the excitement of another's wedding, you may have to fight back the tears or try to whip up some enthusiasm. You may wonder, "But why not me? What's wrong with *me?*" And it doesn't help if you catch the bouquet.

Your peers shape your perception of singleness. Look over this list of personalities:

- *Encouragers*—encourage you
- *Teasers*—generally married, find your singleness amusing
- *Discouragers*—individuals who leave the impression that soon you'll be married and then you can consider yourself whole
- *Achievers*—are preoccupied with their own success

- *Hedonists*—are friends who have adopted an "eat, drink, and be merry" attitude. If you can't be married, you can have a good time! Party! Party!
- *Alumni*—some people, once married, forget your friendship. Occasionally, the one you thought would be your friend *now* has little time for you. That's to be expected.

Ultimately, the problem is not with your friends. It is with you. You need to have plenty of friends, not just a few, because friendships shift, change, stagnate, grow, mature, even fizzle out. And if you put all your eggs into one basket, what are you going to do if they get transferred to Mobile, Alabama?

Ideally, we're not grouped in two camps: married vs. single. Yet, some people (both married and single) act as if it were that way. The most important thing about me is my adulthood, not the nakedness of my ring finger.

So, what can you do when friends marry?

1. Celebrate with them
2. Encourage them to get premarital counseling
3. Give them a great shower
4. Pray for them

That two people wish to sail, in the midst of so many shipwrecked boats, is a dramatic sign of courage. Some skeptics thought Isabella had wasted her investment in Christopher Columbus. Yet—

Besides, in these days, anyone can live together. It takes an act of courage to marry.

But what if you have problems with their engagement? What if you think it's premature or hasty? What should you do? Dare to risk the friendship to confront them. If you don't deal with your concerns, how will you feel if the marriage should fail?

1. Make a time to talk when you won't be interrupted—a good meal is a helpful setting
2. Focus on the issues rather than emotions
3. Express your affirmation for the individual

4. Pray that God will pave the way
5. Suggest postponement or resources

Finally, be generous. Buy a neat card, add a personal note, and buy a special gift. Special doesn't mean expensive, but something that reflects the uniqueness of the couple and the nature of your friendship.

Weddings have a way of encouraging relationships among friends. Some couples have turned the fire under their romance from low to high because friends were getting married. Remember, you're talking about a lifetime commitment. Give your relationship time.

Finally, some of your friends may be *drainers*. Their negativism contaminates everything, including you, so, where two or three are gathered, a pity party erupts.

You may have to limit your time with people who dislike singleness and their singleness in particular.

This has been a problem in some single adult groups or fellowships. One or two couples announce their engagements. Suddenly, the race is on. In fact, some groups become "good places" to meet "someone," but if you're not dating, you'll feel left out.

Singleness is a great season to build and strenthen relationships and friendships. You don't have to have friends your mate likes. So, use this season and enjoy your old friends and make some new ones.

YOUR FAITH

To the [single] who pleases him, God gives wisdom, knowledge and happiness (Eccles. 2:26a, NIV).

But what am I to do with the reality that there are 7,266,000 more single women than single men?*

---

*Statistical abstract of the U.S.: 1985, 105th ed. (Washington: U.S. Government Printing Office, 1985), p. 37 (eighteen and older excludes the military).

"You don't believe in God!" the woman shrieked.

"Yes, ma'am, I do. They wouldn't have me speaking at this conference if I didn't."

"Well, you don't believe in a prayer-answering, miracle-working God."

"Oh, but I do."

"Well, I believe getting a husband is just a matter of prayer. God will give you the desires of your heart. And I want a man."

The theology of mate-seeking begins early in life, as soon as little girls are flower girls and boys are ring bearers. "Someday when I'm grown up, Mommie says I'll be a bride."

It is reinforced in youth groups, "Girls, be true, God has someone picked out for you." Well, I used to believe that.

We like the matchmaking God, *Deus ex* "matchma-kerus." Many times couples have convinced themselves that their relationship was "God's will." Even wedding invitations can use God-talk: "Because God has brought our children together, Mr. and Mrs. _____ invite you. . . ." Some of those weddings couldn't be God's will. A loving God would never so mismatch people.

The idea is historic. Colonial "old maids" placed their shoes at night in the form of a T. Then they marched around the bed three times, repeating: "Placing my shoes, O Lord, in the form of a T, hoping my true love tonight to see." Legend had it that the woman would then see her intended in a dream. No doubt that led to a few nightmares, as well.

What about the desires of our heart? What about the woman who says, "I was made to be married."

I believe that God's *first* desire for us is to be Kingdom-seekers. Some counter, "But with the man comes the Plan! The *two* of us will be God's dynamic duo." I wonder.

Years ago, from a prison cell, Dietrich Bonhoeffer rethought his relationship with his fiancée. He realized that he would probably never live to see her again. After all, he had been involved in the plot to assassinate Hitler. Bonhoeffer could have married her earlier, but he knew "the cost of discipleship." Bonhoeffer rejected a cheap grace that makes God whatever we want him to be.[1] Thus God cannot become a cosmic Santa Claus who provides eternal room service. Costly grace makes us what he wants us to be.

If God is a matchmaker and if Scripture is inspired, how could Paul have written to the Corinthians—of all people—to not get married? Not just once did Paul say that, but four times. When I was a child, if my dad repeated himself, I knew I had better pay attention. Perhaps Paul was running short of lines. Or needed a line or two to make his letter come out the right length.

God allows us the freedom to choose a mate. We bring our choice to the altar and ask God to bless us. Otherwise, if the relationship doesn't work out, we could say to God, "Hey, it's all your fault. You picked her out. I didn't!"

Reality insists that God is the God of *all* truth. He's as much the God of statistics as the God of biology.

Back to my friend whom I mentioned earlier. I took off my shoe and said, "This is a right shoe, isn't it?" She nodded. "To have a *pair* of shoes, you have to have a right *and a left,* agreed?" She again nodded. "But if there are 7,266,000 more *right* shoes than left, you're not going to have pairs unless you put two right shoes together."

"You're trying to trick me. My God can work miracles!" she announced and walked off.

God is committed to our best. " 'For I know the plans I have for you,' declares the Lord, 'plans to prosper you and not to harm you, plans to give you a hope and a future' " (Jer. 29:11, NIV). Now, take out the *you* and insert your name. For I know the plans I have for _____, plans to prosper _____, not to harm _____, plans to give

_____ a future and a hope. And I think that God often adds an exclamation mark.

I sometimes suspect that the super-pious, Bible-totin', Bible quoting singles are not as committed to God's will as they are to God-talk, spiritual clichés, and words.

Allen Hadidian expressed it well: "Often, I have to admit that I am more interested in a change of circumstances than I am in experiencing the sufficiency of Christ." Hadidian also observed:

> We say, "Marriage." God says, "My grace." We say, "I cannot handle this weakness." God says, "My power is perfected in your weakness." We say, "I want a change of circumstances." God says, "I want a change of perspective."[2]

Great singles have learned that marriage is not *the* ultimate. Jesus is!

The second problem with the super-pious singles is that God doesn't always work on their timetable. They become impatient, and suddenly, X doesn't look so bad, especially when an aunt is whispering, "At your age, you shouldn't be so picky."

Men too are attracted by God-talk. They have learned to use the jargon. Jesus and Paul warned about men who work their ways on weak women.

I have not forgotten a breakfast conversation. A woman advised a single friend of mine, "Set a date. Pick out a dress. Leave the rest to God!"

To the single adult who pleases him, God gives wisdom, knowledge, and happiness.

"And?" you gesture impatiently. "Is that all?"

God does not necessarily give a mate, but to all he gives himself.

Actually, it's a choice. How are you praying?

PAUL'S AGENDA————9

LEARN TO BE CONTENT

*I have learned the secret of being content in any and
every situation (Phil. 4:12b, NIV).*

Contentment is learned, not inherited.

Too many single adults miss out on opportunities to
grow because they're locked into *the formula:*
If only I were married, *then* I'd be happy.
If only I were thinner, *then* I'd be happy.
If only I were better educated, *then* I'd be happy.
If only I were prettier, *then* I'd be happy.
If only I'd lose weight, *then* I'd be happy.
If onlys sabotage our singleness. Paul, as a single adult,
said, "I have learned the secret of being content in *any*
and every situation." Paul penned these words in a day
when there were no single adult groups, single adult
newsletters or magazines, single adult life-styles or
apartment complexes.
Paul's world was marriage-oriented, ark-centric and
Jews were expected to marry and to have as many
children as possible. Yet, Paul dared to put singleness on
an equal status with marriage. He acknowledged, "Are
you unmarried? Do not look for a wife." Some singles are

quick to quote that. But Paul continued, "If you do marry, you have not sinned." Yet, in honesty Paul had to add, "But those who marry will face many troubles in this life, and I want to spare you this" (I Cor. 7:27-28, NIV).

Let's take a closer look. Paul said, "I have learned *the secret*" rather than "I have learned to be content." Paul became content through learning, some of which had to be painful. There will be pain, perhaps anguish, at some point in your singleness—the death of a mate or a broken engagement, the loss of a job, the death of a parent. Whatever our pain, we have the chance to ask, "What can I learn from this?"

Many times we moan, "Lord, if it's all the same to you, I'd rather not go through the wilderness." Or "I'd rather skip the unpleasant and get on with the ecstatic."

I recently saw a cartoon that illustrated this point. A mean grouch stood menacingly over a group of slaves who were rowing a boat. One had raised his hand, "Excuse me, but I think I'm getting a blister!" Some of our experiences produce emotional/spiritual blisters before they produce growth.

Or as they say at my health club, "No pain—no gain!"

Yes, there are secrets to be learned.

In Vienna is a cathedral called the Church of the Votives. It doesn't attract many tourists because it is so ugly. Yet, inside the cathedral, visitors are overwhelmed by the stained-glass. Stained-glass cannot be made out of whole sheets of glass; but it is made out of broken pieces, even slivers. "Learning the secret to be content" is to our experience what stained-glass is to windows. Broken pieces of glass make beautiful windows *when* designed by a skilled craftsman.

Second, Paul said, "In any and every situation." There will come those intersections in your singleness that demand your best. The situation may cause you to abandon the traditional answers and to come up with a fresh perspective.

Take a moment to read II Corinthians 11:23-28. How many of those crises could you survive? These were the labs in which Paul's contentedness was shaped. It's one thing to be single in a nice apartment or luxury condo but quite another to be single in a prison cell.

You must share with others what you have learned. Single adult fellowships offer a setting for sharing the road maps. In my case, I went through my divorce cold turkey. Now groups of people who have been through divorce come together to share and to help others survive and thrive.

God expects us to share with others the comfort we have received. Since your experience or perspective will not translate into everyone's life, you need to be cautious in sharing. You need to discipline your tendency to rush in and declare martial law.

Sometimes singleness is the pits. But, by being patient in "any and every situation" we avoid further complications and even worse consequences.

At what point will you befriend your singleness? At what point will you realize that while the grass appears greener on the other side of the fence, according to Derric Johnson, it is greener *where it is watered*.

A popular chorus notes, "In his time, in his time, he makes all things beautiful, *in his time*."

That's possible even with singleness.

Do you want to know why you should be content as an unmarried adult? Well, contented singleness is an apprenticeship that leads to contented adulthood, whether married or single. Simply, you're not ready to be married until you're content in your singleness. Singleness is not a prison sentence to be served with time off for good behavior. It's a way of living this particular stage of your adulthood.

LEARN TO DEVOTE . . . TO DOING GOOD

*[Single adults] must learn to devote themselves to
doing what is good (Titus 3:14a, NIV).*

No one gets more than twenty-four hours in a day.

Despite those who snarl that "life isn't fair," everyone, whether single or married, adult or child, gets sixty minutes to the hour and twenty-four hours to the day.

It's what we do with those sixty minutes that makes a difference. How do you use your time, especially the time spent waiting for Prince/Princess Charming to show up?

Often, married people ask me, "How do you get so much published?" Well the obvious answer is that I have more time to write. As I told one colleague, "I don't spend time waiting in malls for my wife to shop."

A summer ago, in Greece and Yugoslavia, I chuckled at the husbands in our tour group who were always waiting for their wives. I joked that their main exercise was "reaching for their wallets."

I am amazed at how much time single adults waste watching television. For some television is an emotional nite-lite. For most, it saps time. Do you turn it on, first thing in the morning? Do you go to sleep with Johnny Carson or David Letterman? Some single adults turn it on as soon as they get up or come home from work. Indeed, many married couples have stopped talking because of television. They spend time together, all right—in front of the television, grunting during commercials. The intruder in some marriages is not another person but a T.V.

Paul pops our excuse for wasted time. He doesn't say to do good but "*learn* to devote ourselves." Learning implies reexamining our priorities. In my doctoral work

I was required to keep time logs, divided into thirty-minute segments. What a pain! Suddenly, I knew where my time was going and more importantly how it was being wasted.

Oh, I hasten to add, it wasn't bad things. For example, I was stunned by how much time I spent browsing in bookstores. I could argue that as a writer, I was merely checking out the work of my colleagues. Yet, the total of those hours could have produced some significant writing on my part.

Community service offers single adults the chance to participate in something bigger than themselves. Community service is an investment. Havinghurst identified this as one of the major signs of adulthood. He reasoned that now I have children, I am concerned about playgrounds, schools.

But should we wait until we have children?

Second, by giving of ourselves, we often receive far more. Sandy, who volunteered to work in a home for senior adults, responded, "I've been stunned. They have so much to give. I always come home on cloud nine!"

I think of May Smith, a nurse in Dallas, who became concerned about mortality rates for infants in hospitals. So in 1913, she borrowed a tent from the American Red Cross and pitched it on the lawn of Parkland General Hospital in Dallas to start the Dallas Babies Hospital. Thousands of babies have survived because of procedures developed in that hospital.

I think of Ima Hogg who devoted herself to the community through art collecting. Now thousands of Texans delight in viewing her collection.

But, in giving, many single adults have also expanded their social outlets and developed a network of friendships and relationships that have been enriching. Some people have met a future spouse not in front of the television but in doing good or doing volunteer work. Many single adults use their talent in community choruses or opera companies, in ballet troupes, or in community playhouses.

I think of one man in Wichita who dons a clown costume and visits children's hospital wards on holidays.

This ministry of help is important. It diffuses the poor-me syndrome. We need to be available. Have you ever moved and have called for some "strong backs" to help?

"This Friday, huh. Man, wouldn't you know it? I have a softball game. I'd like to help *but*—"

A long-established cliché has been: want something done, give it to a busy person.

You've perhaps seen the cereal commercial where the older child says, "Give it to Mikey. He'll eat anything."

Susan Annette Muto in her fine book, *Celebrating the Single Life,* warns about the chairperson who thinks the single adult unhampered by family life and therefore expects that person to be available "at the drop of a hat." For example, Muto acknowledges that some parents overrely on single sons and daughters. They impose on them because they do not wish to bother a married son or daughter. "We can only care for others in committed service when we temper availability and avoid depleting overwork. In other words, our saying no to people at certain times must be for the sake of a greater yes."[1]

Generally, you have the right to say no just as much as any other adult, especially if after saying yes you are going to feel resentful or angry.

You need to ask, "Does *this* opportunity have my initials on it?" If it does, am I willing to fully invest in it? Many have missed the best by embracing the mediocre.

Opportunities for doing good come to all single adults. Our challenge is to be prepared to discern what is the best and to embrace it.

Doing good is what led Raoul Wallenberg to put aside his personal safety to rescue 100,000 Hungarian Jews from the Nazis during World War II.

Doing good for you may be undramatic, unrecognized, unrewarding. Perhaps even your motives will be questioned. But by devoting yourself to doing what is good, you could and can make a difference.

LEARN TO CONTROL

Each of you should learn to control his own body in a way that is holy and honorable, not in passionate lust like the heathen (I Thess. 4:4-5a, NIV).

Americans are not known for their self-control. "I can't believe I ate the whole thing," moans a man in a commercial. Another popular commercial focuses on the taunt: "Bet you can't eat just one [potato chip]." It's feast or fast; binge or diet. Diet books are consistent best sellers. Why? Americans cannot come to terms with moderation.

Yet, Paul is not amused with the "I just couldn't help myself" or "I couldn't say no." When singles read his words about "passionate lust," they think hormones. But, Paul used a broader brush here.

Perhaps, you've seen the cookie ads on television or seen packages of them on your grocer's shelves. Well, I doubted the commercials. Store-bought cookies couldn't be *that* good, so, on a lark, I bought a bag, just to disprove the commercials. I ate the entire bag of cookies in one sitting.

I was disgusted with myself for a week. But they are *wonderful* cookies! This is the guy who is in such control that he hasn't missed a day of jogging in four years, sabotaged by store-bought cookies.

All single adults have control problems (those without direct control problems have difficulty controlling their pride). Let's consider the problem areas.

● *Food.* That's my weakness. The more calories, the better. If I don't want to be overweight, I have to be in control. That means I avoid Aisle 7 (cookies). I know if I get the item home, I've lost the battle. That means I avoid shopping when I am hungry. That means I am alert to empty calories. For example, a tablespoon of peanut butter (forget the Ritz) is about 100 calories. Yet, a stick of candy may have 100 calories. Which is a *better* 100 calories? Obviously, the peanut butter because of the protein.

It's tempting to whip up a few thousand calories on a dateless night! And that's another benefit of singleness. If there is only one piece of pie left: it's all mine.

However, Paul would urge control.

● *Sex*. We live in a sex-saturated society. Sex is used to sell everything from toothpaste to detergent. Maybe you keep finding yourself giving in. Try rehearsing no or *no!* Some single adults have the notion that it's not as wrong if you go down fighting. However, an ounce of prevention is worth a pound of cure.

Lack of control in sexual matters means there is a drastic shortage of intimacy. Control begins with admitting your sexual needs rather than denying them. Almost all single adults come equipped with hormones, but it is a question of disciplining those needs and drives.

● *Work*. All work and no play makes Bill a dull single adult. Because I have no family, I am constantly tempted to overwork. Work is one acceptable way of compensating for my dull social life, but it can lead me into workaholicism which would further depress my social life.

● *Impulse Buying*. Sometimes, I cannot buy what I want because I'm a good impulse buyer. I found that my department store bills dropped when I put my plastic in a safety deposit box. I realize people are paid good money to create ads, displays, and incredible sales. No wonder some trainers insist, "Salesmanship doesn't begin until the customer says no." I need to constantly ask, "Do I *really* need this?"

- *Mouth.* James says, "No man can tame the tongue." That is an ageless truth. Thirty seconds of silence would solve many disputes. "I wish I hadn't saids" are troublesome.

I confess to being strongly opinionated. If people ask what I think, I am tempted to give them their money's worth. But a controlled single adult *thinks* before he or she speaks.

- *Emotions.* Snow-ball relationships develop because of a lack of control. Hormonal flood tide encourages rapid relationships. Too often people are in love with being in love. They make premature emotional commitments. I've always had trouble saying, "I love you," but, a few friends have said it once too easily.

Many single adults have not been able to grow as adults because of their emotion swings. Certainly, you do not have to be an emotional Scrooge, but it does help to keep your emotions in check.

The disciplined life can be freeing. With discipline many single adults find freedom. Think about a waiter trying to sell you dessert. "It's really good," he says. You can easily afford the $2.75 for a slice of pie. You need to ask, "Who's in charge here: the waiter or me?" But what if he rolls the dessert cart to your table? What if everyone is having dessert? Can you still make your *no* stick?

No is a good and noble word.

Control is a good attitude.

Either you control it or your "its" control you.

I have relied on the string system. I have avoided desserts for several months. Every day makes my will power stronger because, if I give in, I have to start over again with day one.

Paul encouraged his readers to control their bodies. That is a high priority for successful single adult living today, and little lessons pay big dividends.

UNDERSTANDING THE SINGLE ADULT MALE——10

The images that are carried about are burdensome, a burden for the weary (Isa. 46:1b, NIV).

"Isn't that just like a man!"

"What a *man!*" is one of the most coveted evaluations in our society. Men seek it from other men as well as from women. Certainly, sex roles are defined by what the significant others in a man's life regard as appropriate sexual responses for each gender.

However, we have assumed inaccurately that these develop during adolescence. With the strong influence of television, more boys claim they want to be like a certain movie star than their father.

A male is continuously evaluating what the models in his life are doing. Three focal dimensions of the "macho" male are: sexual exploitation and conquest of women, drinking (and to a growing degree violence), display of material goods.

Adolescence is a period to begin pulling away from one's parents in order to develop one's personality to a degree sufficient to ensure survival on one's own. Because of overcontrol, one may rebel. However, no small number rebel in order to get a response out of a parent; in essence, to see if the parent cares. In Belize, the people describe this male as that of the "half-man, half-boy."

In some families, the young males demonstrate (or imitate on a lesser scale) what they see modeled by their fathers or the significant males in their lives. In other families this develops because of the tension of over-maternal control or influence.

Unfortunately, gross remnants of the double standard still persist among evangelicals. Drinking is often a badge of masculinity and movies often portray this. No small number of men drink to go along with peer pressure or to avoid teasing.

The display of material goods (cars, clothes, electronic gear) influences a male's priorities. *Playboy* magazine has contributed to this craze with its what-to-buy advice. Men also take note of the cost and brand names, particularly in hi-fi equipment, often believing bigger is better.

Two hundred years ago, a man's faith was linked to his material blessings; prosperity was a sign of election. In our affluence, we suspect it is the money that one "throws away" that wins macho esteem.

Jesus said, "A man's life does not consist in the abundance of his possessions," (Luke 12:15c, NIV). He had only his robe and often "no place to lay his head" (Luke 9:58). What about Jesus' response to the man who tore down his barn to build a larger one?

We compare ourselves to other Americans, but the poorest American is wealthy by world standards. Our wealth is to be a vehicle or conduit to meet the needs of others.

As Ken Smith observed, "A man does not become a man by bulging muscles, or fighting wars or fathering children. A man becomes a man by becoming what God wants him to be!"[1]

Macho-linity can be a ready-made, permanent press suit of armor for the man recently divorced or widowed, or for those in mid-life transition. Perhaps, you've met the male forty-five going on seventeen with four gold chains, shirt unbuttoned to the navel, and toupee in place. Many men feel they must recapture their youth rather than take advantage of their maturity. As Grandma Walton used to say, "There's no fool like an old fool!"

Macho burns out men. Often they do not realize that they are victims of the world's shallow standards. The malady is seldom terminal, but it does leave welts on the spirit of a man.

Fortunately, social scientists are discovering the danger of macho. Herb Goldberg wrote a book, *The Hazards of Being Male* (Nash Publishing, 1976). A new generation of men could be termed androgynous, not bisexual or asexual, but males "who can slip comfortably out of traditional roles and be themselves. Men can cry and feel dependent without being less male." Research published in the *Ladies' Home Journal* noted that although today's women date obsessive machos, they want to marry supportive, communicating men.[2]

Paul's words are still significant. "See to it that no one takes you captive through hollow and deceptive philosophy, which depends on human tradition and the basic principles of this world" (Col. 2:8, NIV).

THE JABEZ
SYNDROME———————11

"PLEASE BE WITH ME IN ALL THAT I DO"

Whatever your hand finds to do, do it with all your might (Eccles. 9:10a, NIV).

God is interested in everything we do.

Many single adults live out their lives preoccupied with the search for a mate. The selection process is the chief barometer of their value. If the search has not been successful, if it at least appears rewarding, the single adult feels good. If the pursuit has bogged down, the single adult feels depressed.

I have not forgotten three funerals I attended in 1978 while I was on the staff of Point Loma College in San Diego. Three students died between January and June, one only a week from graduation. Christian colleges are not really set up to deal with death. Rather, the focus is on life *after* graduation and/or survival until you get the degree, so many concluded that life begins *after* graduation. No wonder it's called *commence*ment.

What can be said at the death of a single adult? Life was seemingly snuffed out prematurely. I remember the words of our college chaplain, "If I knew what to say I'd say it. If I knew what to sing, I'd sing it." Even our spiritual leader struggled with the tragedies.

Yet, the strong reality was that those three students were not waiting for life to begin. They had already experienced the good life. They were growers. That reality made the funerals a little easier.

Our life agenda is the same, regardless of the stage or our age—to seek the kingdom of God. The particulars may vary at different stages or junctions, but we're committed to being Kingdom-seekers.

Single adults do not compartmentalize their lives neatly into the sacred and the secular as though God were interested in the religious but not overly concerned with the rest of life. Jabez challenged such thinking. He daringly asked God to bless "in every thing that I do." Jabez imposed no boundaries on God's blessings.

What about you? Are you compartmentalized? Are there areas in your life in which you have erected no trespassing signs and have suggested that that includes God?

How many single adults are afraid of God intruding on their search? Of God challenging their carefully constructed agendas? Of God redesigning their tasks? Of God refocusing their priorities?

If we understand God as Creator, can we comprehend that he is interested, not casually or out of curiosity, but actively interested? He is interested in you. He thinks of you continually.

So why not give God a chance to show his interest?

Joseph had lived in his father's house, in a pit, in a prison cell, and at last in a palace. But there were two right turns: *go back two spaces.* In one case he helped a fellow prisoner and expected a reward; Joseph languished in jail until the prisoner remembered.

Yet, this observation in Scripture encourages me, "The Lord was with Joseph and gave him success *in whatever* he did" (Gen. 39:23, NIV, italics added).

The arena in which we are successful may be a prison cell or a palace. The Lord's love for Joseph was not determined by his zip code. In each locale—pit-prison-palace—God was interested; never did he abandon Joseph.

Americans are proud of being self-motivated. We praise self-starters and the self-made individual. Some of us do not wait and learn, we charge full speed ahead. Under our breath we mumble, "God helps those who help themselves."

However, God helps those who *rely on him,* those who are sensitive to his timing, his direction, and his priorities.

In our singleness, God is committed to cheering us on. To observing our development and progress. I suspect that God carries pictures of us in his wallet like a proud papa.

But that also means that at times he has to nudge us off those dead centers that seem so attractive.

God, the Creator, longs for us to share the details of our lives. Life is not unlike a coloring book. God is concerned about the colors we choose, whatever they might be.

Perhaps you recall your coloring experiences. Sometimes an adult usurped authority and cramped your creative process.

"You can't color her face green!" the adult snapped.

"Oh, yeah, why not?" No wonder children lose most of their creativity by age seven when adults answer, "Just because."

Our text suggests, "*Whatever* your heart finds to do, do it with all your might."

Chariots of Fire won a basket of Oscars in 1983. Millions of people cheered in darkened theaters as Eric Liddell ran his race. Yet it was his words that moved us deeply, "I feel his pleasure when I run."

In everything "do it with all your might." That you too may "feel his pleasure" just as Eric Liddell did.

"AND HELP ME IN MY WORK"

Your plenty will supply what they need (II Cor. 8:14, NIV).

Our work, whatever it is, is to reflect God's glory. Yet, Millie, a thirty-six-year-old never-married, hates her job. She is a legal secretary, locked into routine and habit. While the job pays well it leaves her restless. Everything is so predictable. Every Monday is exactly like the previous Monday.

Her friend Kim had the same problem. Over sack lunches, snatching noontime sun, watching men, cruising stores for blue-light specials, naturally they discussed the "if onlys" of their jobs.

They had to admit that their jobs financed a good life-style—new cars, credit cards, ski weekends, a condo. They had few economic problems that other single adults in their fellowship had.

Finally, opportunity knocked. Kim became a volunteer for the Billy Graham Crusade. Typing after work, filing with incredible efficiency. The director praised her work, "Kim, I'd love to have you on our permanent staff, but," he laughed, "we couldn't begin to match your salary." He had planted a seed in Kim's mind.

Two months after the Crusade, Kim turned in her resignation and went to work full time with the Graham organization at a fraction of her former income.

When I last visited with her, I asked, "How's it going?" For an hour Kim shared, from a happy heart. She had no regrets, not even on payday.

Your work, whatever it is, is to reflect God's glory. Single adults are big on work. The Protestant work ethic of our Puritan forefathers is alive and well among most single adults, especially single women. Once women were confined to teaching school, nursing, or typing. Now, they are accountants, managers, attorneys, judges. The barriers have been eroded. The sky's the limit. Go for it!

Historically, single adults were viewed by businessmen as unstable and insecure. Why weren't they married? Promotions were denied or directed to married candidates. One national insurance firm still promotes single adults only so far in their organization. Then it is either marry—stagnate—or leave.

Yet, other companies prefer single adults. Suppose a company wants to transfer an employee to Syracuse. It has two candidates: John—married, three children, wife with good job; and Bill—unmarried. John would need three to six months to effect a move.

Bill, however, can move within two weeks, at a fraction of the cost of moving John *and his family*. Emotionally, it is easier to move Bill. Suppose John moves and his wife hates Syracuse? They fight about it, and soon John's productivity is affected.

Second, singles can remain after work or be more flexible. They don't have families waiting for them.

Generally a job offers the single adult the opportunity to earn enough money to buy the affluent singles' life-style. You may hate your job but boredom becomes comfortable because you're fantasizing about your new car or the ski weekend.

Single adults also experience work stress. Perhaps, there's a correlation with the happy hour at the singles' bar after work. The compromises, the frustrations, the bureaucracies, the red tape—all create stress that exists long after the work day is over. Some single adults in moments of honesty ask, "Is it *really* worth it?"

Perhaps you're one of those singles who would like to quit your job but are afraid of the risk. You stay with your job and your effectiveness diminishes; your resentment increases. However as long as paychecks come twice a month and a bonus at Christmas, you survive.

Probably you can't just up and quit, but you can develop a strategy for changing a job or refurbishing your attitudes about your present job. Barbara Sher has written an excellent book that can help you change your attitude about your job. It's called *Wishcraft: How to Get What You Really Want.* The book is not a glorification of the me-first thinking or an endorsement of the survival of the fittest. Rather she offers effective strategies for making real change, and for converting vague yearnings into reality and challenging jobs.

She related the story of Diane, who wanted to be a city planner. Diane started her career by attending block-association parties in the evening *after work.* Sher concluded, "If your goal is to make your living by doing what you love, start doing it just for love." Diane gained practical experience that made her a preferred candidate over those with equal technical expertise.[1]

Your job must not become your god, your status symbol. Rather, your job is to be a conduit through which God allows you to gain resources to be shared with others. This is why Paul said, "Your plenty will supply what they need." It's tempting to pray, "O Lord, help Sally. You know that her ex is a bona fide low-life and is three months behind in alimony. And she can't attend the retreat this weekend."

But the Lord whispers, "Why don't *you* do something about Sally's needs." So you increase the volume of your prayer, "O Lord, help Sally."

I remember a line of a song from my childhood: "O to be his hand extended, reaching out."

Many jobs are perceived as secular. We have divided Christians into the ordained and the unordained. A single adult sometimes explains, "I'm *just* a layperson." That hardly represents a biblical perspective. All of us are called. Our jobs, whatever they are, are ordained by God to be instrumental in bringing about his kingdom. Katherine Lackman said it well in *Arkenstone:* "As I see it, I am required to do my work, whatever it is, as diligently and caringly as Jesus would have done the same job had he chosen my profession for a while."[2]

How would Jesus handle your job, your colleagues, your pressures, your temptations?

Finally, a word about Prince/Princess Charming's job. Maybe you are saving yourself for a doctor (because in our society that is instant status) or a professional. Unfortunately, job snobbery exists among some singles. I meet people who are impressed that I am a writer and speaker. But what if I were a truck driver or garbage collector? Would they still be as interested in me?

Prince/Princess Charming may not wear designer suits and dresses. Prince/Princess Charming may have calloused hands, but the real question should be, Whatever their profession, do they possess integrity?

"AND KEEP ME FROM EVIL AND DISASTER"

Have no fear of sudden disaster or the ruin that overtakes the wicked (Prov. 3:25, NIV).

It's a great cartoon. In the cartoon Cathy's parents are second-guessing their daughter's security. Cathy's father is wondering if she has locked up. That irritates Cathy's mother who scolds him, "Oh for heaven's sake, you remind her to lock up 400 times a week!" Then she proceeds to worry aloud about keeping the roast beef wrapped up. Then her father counters with, "I wonder if she's checked the batteries in the smoke detector."

The last frame of the cartoon finds both parents on Cathy's doorstep with a benevolent grim, "We thought of a worry we could agree on."

On occasion there are those 11:00 P.M. "just wanted to see if everything's O.K." phone calls. It's as if an announcer has demanded: "It's eleven o'clock. Do you know where you single son or daughter is?" After all there are rapes, muggings, robberies, and miscellaneous but minor disasters to stimulate parental worry.

Indeed, one of the motivations for marriage is security. Many parents have breathed easier when their son/daughter was in another's custody. I admit that when one is married and hears "thump! thump!" in the night, it is a secure feeling to have someone else to investigate.

Sonny and Cher used to sing, "I Got You, Babe." Yet, the rising number of divorces following a crisis demonstrates that a mate may not be there through thick and thin.

I think of Brenda, whose husband left her when she gave birth to a child with Downs syndrome.

I think of Bill, whose wife left him the day after their youngest child got married.

I think of Lynn, whose husband had divorce papers served on her the day he graduated from law school.

We are bombarded by tragedies. The constant reporting of evening news keeps us more alert than our grandparents were. In those days it sometimes took a week to get news of a tragedy. Now we feel overwhelmed with tragedies, disasters, crises, and chaos.

However, you will eventually have to come to terms with disaster-anxiety. Our confidence comes in our commitment to God, who does not exempt us from crises or disasters but accompanies us through those experiences. Indeed, as Paul declared, nothing can separate us from his love. It may be unpleasant, unfair, but we will survive.

Our forefathers sang these words of the great hymn, "How Firm a Foundation":

> When through the deep waters I call thee to go,
> The rivers of woe shall not thee overflow;
> For I will be with thee thy trials to bless,
> And sanctify to thee thy deepest distress.

And many single adults would nod in agreement with those words. Our "deepest distress" is survivable.

SERVANTHOOD————12

THE NEW FRONTIER

Serve one another in love (Gal. 5:13c, NIV).

One who has no time to be a servant will have no time to become a saint.

It's difficult to get good help these days. I suspect that even the Lord would agree with that statement. Many single adults want dramatic ministries. Just don't ask me to be a servant.

I think, however, of Florence Nightingale. How desperately she wanted to nurse wounded soldiers. That was what God had called her to do. Yet, military bureaucrats kept her and her nurses at bay; meanwhile, the soldiers suffered and died. Finally, she volunteered to scrub floors. The death rate at Scutari dropped from 40 percent to less than 3 percent. Some soldiers thought of their hospital as a church because of the godly influence of Florence.[1] Thousands of men survived because her nurses weren't afraid to be servants.

Admittedly, servanthood probably won't get *you* on the cover of *Time*. Only one Mother Teresa per decade. Yet, Mother Teresa is a servant because she sees Jesus in the face and broken body of each patient.

Paul, the greatest missionary of all time, considered himself a servant, yet, a thankful servant. Numerous times Paul took time to praise those who had assisted him. Just look at the last chapter of each of his letters.

When Paul found himself shipwrecked and in a perfect position to say, "I told you so," he gathered firewood instead and suffered a snakebite as a result. He chose not to sit around.

There are thousands of single servants, known only to the heart of God. I think of Maylou Thompson, a music professor who influenced prominent organist Don Hustaad. Maylou's mother, when dying, said, "Take care of your father." Maylou tried to get her father to move to the city where she was teaching.

"No," he responded. "I won't leave my farm." So Maylou gave up her academic post, and for sixteen years she was a servant, caring for her father. Some today would be horrified at her sacrifice, yet for Maylou it was a question of servanthood and obedience.

Servants don't always relish the consequences of obedience. Yet God has his own timetable for rewarding their faithfulness.

I think of Lillian Trasher who spent fifty years running an orphanage in Egypt. In fact, she broke an engagement ten days before her wedding to go. When I researched her life, I had assumed that she was probably homely, but while working in the Archives of the Assemblies of God, I found a picture of her in her twenties. She had been a beautiful woman. Often people pitied her. To their "Poor Lillian," she responded:

> Poor dears, they don't know what they have missed . . . a chance to make over broken lives and to build up the most wonderful memories a girl can have of her youth. . . . There was the joy of repairing crushed lives, of loving dying babies back to life, of spending my life for God. No, it was not a lost youth. Never! Now the memories are golden, priceless and cannot be taken away. . . .
> If the Lord allowed me to live my life over, I would do the same thing for another fifty, another hundred years.[2]

A servant doesn't always emphasize the results. A servant sees a job to be done and attempts to do the best job he or she can. Paul wrote, "Serve one another in love." Many times Paul must have been inconvenienced by his baby believers. Yet, he responded to their needs.

Your singlehood offers a season for servanthood. Lillian Trasher took care of babies—thousands of them in the course of her career. Those babies grew up, and in adulthood they have filled responsible positions in every stratum of Egyptian society. Is it only coincidence that in the Arab world, Egypt remains an American ally? Hardly. I would suggest that Lillian's years demonstrated a servanthood that attributed to the softening of attitudes. I would suggest that the pro-American stance has been influenced to some degree by this great humanitarian's example.

VOLUNTEERS MAKE A DIFFERENCE

Religion that God our Father accepts as pure and faultless is this: to look after orphans and widows in their distress and to keep oneself from being polluted by this world (James 1:27, NIV).

Volunteering is a great way to keep oneself from beng polluted by the idea "let someone else do it."

I am not sure if churches are supposed to have theme songs but when I was growing up in Kentucky, it seems that we closed every youth camp with:

> It may not be on the mountain's height
> Or over the stormy sea;
> It may not be at the battle's front
> My Lord will have need of me.

The chorus simply said, "I'll go where you want me to go, dear Lord."

Well, for me, it hasn't exactly been mountains or vales

or seas. Rather it has been retreat centers, educational units, and motel conference rooms. As a teen I coveted a *major* assignment—to do something big, meaning significant or important in the world's eyes as well as in God's eyes. I had a notion that God had some key assignments—the dramatic, the stupendous, the impossible—that he asked individuals to do.

I thought surely the number-one priority was to be a missionary. That was the highest level of service, and I was willing. In fact, I thought sure I was called. In 1968, I applied for the Student Mission Corps. One spring day, as I returned to my dorm after class, I found a telegram (my first: see, already it was dramatic) with the words, "Will you serve?"

"Will I serve?" Of course! A few days after graduation I was on my way to Belize, feeling quite sacrificial since I had had to miss my roommate's wedding. Ah, the scent of sacrifice.

That brief volunteer stint changed me. When I returned I had a world view as well as a tan, ten sets of film to develop, assorted souvenirs, and stories. Initially, I was angry about what I had experienced. My volunteer trek burst my bubble, particularly about missionaries. After that summer I could not be the same person, because I found out that I didn't have a servant's heart but a grandstander's heart.

That's what volunteering is all about: whether it is stuffing envelopes, or answering telephones during a call-a-thon, or participating in a Work and Witness program. It means interrupting our lives and risking our world views. Volunteering creates both short-term and long-term consequences.

Volunteering has had an incredible impact on American politics and social life.

Today we are conscious of the needs of the mentally ill, but in earlier American history the mentally ill were often housed in jails with common criminals.

In 1841, a young Harvard student realized that he would never be effective as a volunteer teaching a Sunday school class for women inmates at the Cambridge jail, so, he asked a young woman to recommend a replacement. She volunteered.

"But you're already busy," he protested. However, the next Sunday, the new volunteer found her way to the prison, later saying she could smell it before she could see it. From that class began a movement to reform both jails and mental health care. From there, Dorothea Dix traveled through every state lobbying for reform. In one jail, on a cold morning, she asked why an insane woman had no clothes.

"Oh, she don't feel the cold," the jailer chuckled.

"If I am cold, she is cold! Get her a blanket!" Dorothea Dix challenged not only the policies but the thinking (or lack of thinking) behind them.

With the outbreak of the Civil War, Dorothea recognized the need for nurses. She volunteered and found herself appointed superintendent of nursing for the Union Army. As a volunteer, she methodically made a difference.[3]

There seem to be three types of people today.

First are those who are unwilling, who in essence pray, "O Lord, bless my four and no more." They refuse to be touched. In some cases, they feel inadequate or perhaps they tried and failed.

The second class is composed of those who are willing but wait. They wait for the right moment, the invitation, the opportunity. Some excuse this waiting as God's will.

People in the third class are unwilling to wait. They see a need and respond. They do not wait for presentations or position papers or formal announcements. Many times, these people take jobs that are not obvious and for which there is little praise or recognition. I'm thinking of a widow who has an incredible public ministry. She began in the kitchen of her church. She saw that the kitchen had

had one too many suppers, so, she began organizing, cleaning, scouring, but always making time for the people who used (and abused) the kitchen.

God has a way of taking our "cups of cold water" and leading those with a volunteer spirit to progressively tougher tasks.

Dorothea Dix began in a jail with a Sunday school class.

The same is true of the Grimké sisters, Angelina and Sarah, whose volunteer spirit as speakers and writers influenced the passion of the antislavery movement. They did not realize when they volunteered that it would mean dodging rocks and eggs and rotten fruit.

The same is true with those first efforts of volunteer nurses during the Civil War, but as a result the profession of nursing emerged.

The same is true of the first efforts of women in prohibition politics. Francis Willard's band of holy volunteers in the W.C.T.U. produced reform.

Great movements seem so massive, but they generally begin in the heart of a person with a servant's spirit to whom God entrusted a dream and a willingness to tackle at least part of that dream.

Jill Briscoe captured the attitude of many single adults with her book title, *Here Am I—Send Aaron* (Victor Books, 1978).

Some needs have become causes and some have become crusades and soapboxes for individuals with personal agendas and a lust for power and recognition.

Yet, the true volunteer has a servant's heart and spirit. Whether cleaning at the church, teaching a Sunday school class of squirming children, visiting shut-ins, or folding bulletins, the volunteer serves.

The Father who watches the sparrow's flight is aware of the volunteer's vigil—in doing the unrecognized, the unpraised, the unpleasant, the unnoticed. And in that distant morning, the volunteer will hear, "Well done, good and faithful volunteer!"

ACCOUNTABILITY——**13**

WHAT TO DO WHILE WAITING FOR PRINCE/CESS CHARMING

Be wise: make the most of every opportunity (Eph. 5:15-16, TLB).

Tomorrow begins today.

So, you want to know where the tardy prince/cess is? Somehow you suspect that he/she isn't tied up in traffic on the freeway of life.

People will keep asking the question, "When are you going to settle down?" You can count on that.

Waiting for prince/cess does not have to be a time of wasted waiting. It can be a time of anticipatory but productive waiting, not unlike that of a couple expecting a baby. This is the time to develop *your* potential—to stretch, to grow. Admittedly, it may be a time of ambiguities, uncertainties, and ambivalence.

Until the arrival consider the following options:

1. Learn to play a musical instrument.
2. Go to school/go back to school. For example, community colleges offer a wide array of courses for self-improvement. Take a course in communications, drama, or business.

3. Learn a new skill. Learning cake decorating, scuba diving, piloting, skiing, sky diving, hang-gliding, investing, auto repair will give you something to brag about.
4. Visit a dude ranch for a week.
5. Visit the nation's capital.
6. Learn a foreign language. This can also be beneficial as our nation becomes more bilingual. Also this might be a help in a job change or promotion.
7. Become computer proficient. This is a chance to meet a challenge, meet new people, and add to your vocational, marketable skills.
8. Raft the Colorado River.
9. Work in a political campaign. Volunteers are always needed, and it makes you part of something bigger than yourself.
10. Run for political office.
11. Work on a telethon for a charity or other cause.
12. Go on a cruise.
13. Visit a third-world nation through a work and witness team.
14. Go to a wrestling match. If nothing else it will take your mind off your singleness.
15. Sell Tupperware, Amway, or some other product.
16. Volunteer to work in a hospital, orphanage, or nursing home.
17. Learn to hang wallpaper.
18. Adopt a child/support a child.

If none of the above seems interesting, here are others suggested by Ginger Hutton of the *Arizona Republic:*

1. Learn to control your temper.
2. Learn to sit up and chew with your mouth closed.
3. Run a mile each morning and swim a half-mile each afternoon or evening (because it's good for you).[1]

Other suggestions from singles who have tried them are:

1. Take up golf.
2. Get a big dog. Walking it will give you exercise and get you out of the house. Pet owners often strike up conversations with other pet owners.
3. Use your library card. If nothing else it will improve your mind.
4. Join a health club. Health clubs are the new singles' meeting places.
5. Go for a hot air balloon ride. It's great for expanding your perspective.
6. Go on Outward Bound. Learn to climb a mountain.

BLEACHER PEOPLE

Do not let any unwholesome talk come out of your mouths, but only what is helpful for building others up according to their needs, that it may benefit those who listen (Eph. 4:29, NIV).

We singles need bleacher people. We need people who will cheer for us.

It was a muggy spring afternoon, five weeks before graduation. I was enduring fifth period senior English class and another pointless discussion of Byron. I was failing. The prospect of summer school and delayed graduation loomed over my consciousness.

I'm not sure why he said it—anger, frustration. The teacher looked at me and snarled, "Smith, you'll never amount to anything!!!" (I'm sure he used *three* exclamation marks.)

Silence was followed by muffled snickering of my buddies. The teacher sensed my humiliation and moved on.

It took forever for the bell to ring. Finally, I crawled out and cut my sixth period class, assured my buddies were proclaiming the incident to anyone who would listen.

Twenty years have passed. I have never forgotten that teacher's allegation: "Smith, you'll never amount to anything."

Perhaps you have had a similar encounter, maybe with a father, a mother, a husband or wife, an employer, a minister. Perhaps you're still limping emotionally. Your singleness has been handicapped by *the remark*.

Let's face it. Such things happen to good people. Earlier I suggested that it's not so much what happens to us but the way we respond. But some of us, at the moment are too devastated to respond verbally, so, someone has to respond for us. Someone has to help us limp to the finish line.

During my senior year high school football was also a disaster. A school with a winning tradition had a losing season—an awful losing season. I can still remember the post-game tirades. In those days coaches were free to be painfully specific in reviewing our athletic deficiencies.

Then on Monday mornings the non-jocks freely offered their analyses of our loss. Everyone had winning suggestions and strategies. In the afternoon, practice began again to ready us for the next game.

Of course some parents were convinced that if the "idiot coach" were fired or if two more pints of milk were given to us at lunchtime or if "my son" played more we would win. By third quarter each week, fans were heading toward the parking lot in order to get a good seat at the area restaurants for the post-game bashes. The cheerleaders even caved-in by the start of the fourth quarter.

Yet, on some of those cold, late October/early November nights you could hear someone screaming:

> "Hurrah for Butler! Hurrah for Butler!
> Someone's in the bleachers, yelling,
> 'Hurrah for Butler.'
> 1, 2, 3, 4—who you gonna yell for?
> Butler that's who!"

The score didn't matter to the bleacher person. That person didn't cuss or fuss, just simply yelled out encouragement for a good play, a good block. "Way to go, fellas!"

In the midst of our singleness, we need bleacher people.

> "Hurrah for Susan! Hurrah for Susan!"
> "Hurrah for Bill! Hurrah for Bill!"

Part of my single season must be an awareness that others have needs, too. Perhaps my own needs get overlooked, ignored, or easily dismissed. Yet, I have an opportunity to become a bleacher person. That's the real meaning of single adult groups and fellowships.

Sometimes bleacher people have no hint of their effectiveness. My writing career was ignited by an educational psychology professor, John L. Moore. Every day I sat in the back row, kind of listening. He assigned a term paper on the use of comic books in the teaching of reading. I turned in my assignment.

It came back with an A but more importantly a note. "Good paper. Creative. Why don't you sit closer to the front and participate more in class discussion?" I moved and began sharing in class.

John Moore became my bleacher person. He was the one who encouraged me to apply for grad school. He always stood in the wings, applauding and on occasion laughing.

One Thanksgiving Day I lost my bleacher-er. It broke my heart that he died before my novel was finished. But on nights when I'm confused or discouraged or stuck, in my mind's soundtrack I can still hear John chanting, "Hurrah for Harold."

Bleacher people keep screaming, even when others have gone home.

Bleacher people wait around at the locker room door. Sometimes it's a hint of a smile, a slap on the shoulder, or a whisper, "next time."

Simply, bleacher people make a difference.

Singleness offers you a perfect occasion to become a bleacher person. And it heightens your awareness of the need for bleacher people, because you need them too.

THE UNSPEAKABLE JOYS OF SINGLENESS

Sing and make music in your heart to the Lord, always giving thanks to God the Father for everything, in the name of our Lord Jesus Christ (Eph. 5:19b-20, NIV).

There is a joy to be discovered in singleness that cannot be explained—only experienced!

Many single adults moan to one another, "Well, you'll just have to make the best of a bad situation!" Some singles are aware that the alternative to singlehood for them is not good. Many single adults in a moment of weakness, of desperation, of frustration have settled for second best.

Bobbie Reed notes that personal prisons come in a variety of forms. Many have seen singleness as a prison sentence to be served, with time off for good behavior. Reed quickly debunks that myth in her *Making the Most of Single Life*. She hurts for those who are "single and stuck," who are defeated by rejection, fear, loneliness, past failure, or insecurity.

> God has not planned a defeated life for us, but rather a maturing process through which we become conformed to the image of Christ. [Single adults must learn] . . . that the abundant life is not truly experienced by people who just sit back and let things happen! Victorious, growing people get involved in making their lives full and rewarding.[2]

Thus, your agenda, my agenda as a single adult is simple—to make the most of this season called single-ness. To, in Paul's words, "redeem the time." I have no guarantee of a tomorrow but I do have today.

Single adults are pilgrims on a shared destiny—to know Christ in his fullness, to enjoy the abundant life he offers. There is a joy to be discovered in singleness that cannot be explained—only experienced. That joy erupts when we "live purposeful, creative lives oriented toward the pursuit of excellence in our profession and position and toward some kind of service to humanity that ties in with our temperament and talents."[3]

A phrase from the hymn "A Charge to Keep I Have" comes to mind, "To serve the present age, my calling to fulfill."

Take a time out from reading to answer the following questions Alfred Armand Montapert has formulated. Your answers will reflect your understanding of the opportunity of singleness.

- Am I doing the things that make me happy?
- Are my thoughts of noble character?
- How can I simplify my life?
- What are my talents?
- Does my work satisfy my soul?
- Am I giving value to my existence?
- How can I improve my life?[4]

To these I would add, "What keeps me from

experiencing the joy of singleness?" What keeps me from making the most of my single life?

Eartha White was a prominent black social worker in Jacksonville, Florida. She supervised nine projects—including a nursing home and an orphanage—until she was ninety-eight years old. Although her fiancée had died a month before their wedding day, Eartha chose not to live in the past. She chose to seek the abundant life and discovered joy.

Eartha once quoted her mother saying, "Any old dead fish can go down stream, but it takes a live one to swim up!" At age ninety-four she received the Lane Bryant Award given to the "*one* person in American considered to have made the most significant contribution to his/her community." She was selected over five hundred other nominees. Her philosophy of life—originally stated by John Wesley—led to an unspeakable joy:

> Do all the good you can,
> In all the ways you can,
> In all the places you can,
> For all the people you can,
> As long as ever you can.
> *John Wesley*

Despite life's tragedies and burdens, she found that unspeakable joy in singleness.

WHAT ABOUT A MILLION YEARS FROM TODAY?

> "To the [single adults] who keep my Sabbaths, who choose what pleases me and hold fast to my covenant—to them I will give within my temple and its walls a memorial and a name better than sons and daughters" (Isa. 56:4-5a, NIV).

My choices today will influence my tomorrows.

So, we've come to the end of our journey.

We're still single, but, we've stretched.

I see that you have gotten rid of some of that excess baggage. Good for you! Sure there are still some areas that need attention, but in time.

What about one million years from today, from *this* moment? You see we are not mere biochemical blobs destined to appear, then to vanish into nothingness. Hardly. We're people made in the image of God to become all that he has dreamed us to be.

For one million years from this moment, eternity will just have begun. Bruce Larson noted in *No Longer Strangers* (Word, 1985) that God doesn't change us in order to love us, but because he loves us he cannot leave us as we are. Larson suspects that it will take a thousand years or so for some of us to become all that God has intended.

I believe you are unique, that somewhere within you is a dream nugget:

- to write a song or poem or play or book
- to encourage a child
- to heal a wound
- to rekindle hope
- to work for peace
- to make a difference

I hope this book has taken you one step closer to your dream. Your opportunity.

I need you.

This world needs you.

God needs you.

God could have called a band of lone rangers to fulfill his dream. Instead, he called people. He chose adults, both married and single, to make a difference.

NOTES

1. COMMENTS

1. Bureau of the Census, Department of Commerce and Labor, *Marriage and Divorce, 1867–1906: Summary, Laws, and Foreign Statistics,* Part I (Washington, D.C.: U.S. Government Printing Office, 1909), p. 4.

2. Quoted from *The Boston Quarterly Review,* 1859.

3. Lydia Kingsmill Commander, *The American Idea* (New York: A. S. Barnes, 1907), p. 187.

4. Henry James, Horace Greeley, and Stephen Pearl Andrews, *Love, Marriage and the Divorce and Sovereignty of the Individual: A Discussion* (Boston: Benjamin R. Tucker, 1889), p. 187.

5. *Single Blessedness or Single Ladies and Gentlemen Against the Slanders of the Pulpit, the Press and the Lecture Room* (New York: C. S. Francis, 1852), p. 2.

6. J. David Jones, "Single in America," *Solo,* March–April, 1982, p. 37.

7. David P. Starrard, "Changes in the American Family: Fact and Fiction," in *Changing Images of the Family,* ed. Virginia Tufte and Barbara Myerhoff (New Haven: Yale University, 1979), p. 327; Mark A. Noll and Nathan O. Hatch, *The Search for Christian America* (Westchester, Ill.: Crossway Books, 1983), pp. 144-45.

8. Jerome Kagan, *The Nature of the Child* (New York: Basic Books, 1984), xvii.

9. Ellen K. Rothman, *Hands and Hearts: A History of Courtship in America* (New York: Basic Books, 1984).

10. Dorothy Payne, *Singleness* (Philadelphia: Westminster Press, 1983), p. 22.

2. BACKGROUND

1. William E. Phipps, *The Sexuality of Jesus* (New York: Harper & Row, 1973), p. 80.

2. Crane Brinton, *A History of Western Morals* (San Diego: Harcourt Brace Jovanovich, 1959), p. 93.

3. Donald F. Winslow, "Sex and Anti-Sex in the Early Church Fathers" in *Male and Female: Christian Approaches to Sexuality*, ed. Ruth Tiffany Barnhouse and Urban T. Holmes, III (New York: Seabury Press, 1976), p. 29.

4. Frederick W. Farrar, *Lives of the Fathers* (Edinburg: Adam & Charles Black, 1889), pp. 398-99.

5. Winslow, "Sex and Anti-Sex in the Early Church Fathers," p. 32.

6. Dwight Hervey Small, *Christian: Celebrate Your Sexuality* (Old Tappan, N.J.: Fleming H. Revell, 1974), p. 57.

7. "The Apology Against the Books of Rufinus," trans. John N. Hritzu in *Saint Jerome, Dogmatic and Polemical Works*, vol. 53, *The Fathers of the Church* (Washington, D.C.: University of America Press, 1965), pp. 97-98.

8. Bertrand Russell, *A History of Western Philosophy* (London: Allen & Unwin, 1946), pp. 398-99.

9. David R. Mace, *The Christian Response to the Sexual Revolution* (Nashville: Abingdon Press, 1970), pp. 52-53.

10. Winslow, "Sex and Anti-Sex in the Early Church Fathers," p. 37.

11. Mace, *The Christian Response to the Sexual Revolution*, p. 62.

12. Small, *Christian: Celebrate Your Sexuality*, p. 84.

13. Roland H. Bainton, *Erasmus of Christendom* (New York: Scribner Book Companies, 1969), p. 49; Phipps, *The Sexuality of Jesus*, p. 98.

14. John Calvin, *Commentary on the Epistles of Timothy, Titus, and Philemon* (Grand Rapids: Wm. B. Eerdmans, 1948), p. 131.

15. William Graham Cole, *Sex in Christianity and Psychoanalysis* (New York: Oxford University Press, 1955), p. 121.

16. Parke Rouse, Jr., *Planters and Pioneers: Life in Colonial Virginia* (New York: Hastings House, 1968), p. 47.

17. Linda Ford, "William Penn's View on Women: Subjects of Friendship," *Quaker History*, 72, Fall, 1983, pp. 93, 92.

18. Oscar Theodore Balck, Jr., and Hugh Talmadge Tefler, *Colonial America* (New York: Macmillan, 1958), p. 447.

19. Allen D. Chandler, *Colonial Records of the State of Georgia*, vol. III (Atlanta: Franklin Printing, 1906), p. 774.

20. Arthur W. Calhoun, *A Social History of the American Family*, vol. I, *The Colonial Period* (New York: Barnes & Noble, 1917), p. 256.

21. Bernard I. Murstein, *Love, Sex, and Marriage Through the Ages* (New York: Springer, 1974), p. 300; A. Monroe Aurand, *Two-in-a-Bed* (Aurand Press, 1931), p. 38.

22. Oscar Handlin and Lillian Handlin, *A Restless People: Americans in Rebellion, 1770-1787* (New York: Doubleday, 1982), p. 89; Calhoun, *A Social History of the American Family*, vol. II, p. 73.

23. Selma R. Williams, *Demeter's Daughters: The Women Who Founded America, 1587-1792* (New York: Atheneum Publishers, 1976), pp. 241-47.

24. Evelyn Wingo Thompson, *Luther Rice: Believer in Tomorrow* (Nashville: Broadman Press, 1967), p. 52.

25. Calhoun, *A Social History of the American Family*, vol. II, p. 13.

26. Catherine Clinton, *The Plantation Mistress* (New York: Pantheon Books, 1983), p. 60.

27. Calhoun, *A Social History of the American Family,* vol. II, p. 203.

28. John Bakeless, *Background to Glory: Life of George Rogers Clark* (Philadelphia: J. B. Lippincott, 1957), pp. 356, 53.

29. *Single Blessedness,* p. xvii.

30. John Baldwin Buckstone, *Single Life: Comedy in Three Acts* (London: Chapman & Hall, 1840), pp. 9, 14, 25.

31. George Smith, *Henry Martyn: Saint and Scholar* (London: Religious Tract Society, 1892), p. 44.

32. George Ticknor Curtis, *The Life of James Buchanan,* vol. I (New York: Harper & Row, 1883), pp. 19-22.

33. Carl Sandburg, *Abraham Lincoln: The Prairie Years,* vol. I (New York: Harcourt Brace Jovanovich, 1926), p. 227.

34. James T. De Shields, *They Sat in High Place: The Presidents and Governors of Texas* (San Antonio: Naylor, 1940), p. 7.

35. Catherine Clinton, *The Other Civil War: American Women in the Nineteenth Century* (New York: Hill & Wang, 1984), p. 85.

36. Alice Kessler-Harris, *Out to Work: A History of Wage Earning Women in the United States* (New York: Oxford University Press, 1982), pp. 33, 24.

37. David Tyack and Elisabeth Hansot, *Managers of Virtue: Rural School Leadership in America, 1820–1980* (New York: Basic Books, 1982), p. 69.

38. Gerda Lerner, *The Grimké Sisters from South Carlina* (New York: Schocken Books, 1971).

3. ISSUES

1. Mike Yaconelli, "Thou Shalt Have No Other Celebrities Before Thee," *The Wittenburg Door,* December–January, 1983–1984, p. 31.

2. See Harold Ivan Smith, "Hazards to Your Singleness," *Christian Single, March, 1984, pp. 22-23.*

3. *"Eleanor Chestnut,"* in *A Dictionary of Women in Church History,* ed. Mary L. Hammack (Chicago: Moody Press, 1984), p. 33.

4. For more information see Irwin Ross, "Feelings of Inferiority," *Sky,* May, 1980, pp. 70-72; David A. Seamands, *Healing for Damaged Emotions* (Wheaton, Ill.: Victor Books, 1981), pp. 49-54; M. Blaine Smith, *One of a Kind: A Biblical View of Self-Acceptance* (Downers Grove, Ill.: Inter Varsity Press, 1984), p. 48.

5. Dennis Altman, *AIDS in the Mind of America* (New York: Doubleday, 1985), p. 12; William Novak, *The Great American Man Shortage* (New York: Rawson, 1983), p. 38.

6. Art Carey, *In Defense of Marriage* (New York: Walker, 1984), p. 89.

7. Sidney Jourard, *The Transparent Self* (New York: Van Nostrand Reinhold, 1971), p. 59.

8. James Ramey, *Intimate Friendships* (Englewood Cliffs, N.J.: Prentice-Hall, 1976), p. 99.

9. Carey, *In Defense of Marriage,* p. 123.

4. APPROACHES

1. Rosemary Radford Reuther and Rosemary Skinner Keller, eds., *The Colonial and Revolutionary Periods,* vol. II, *Women and Religion in America* (New York: Harper & Row, 1983), p. 293.

2. Payne, *Singleness,* pp. 11-12.

3. Ibid., p. 34.

4. Laurence Alma Tademan, "Little Girls," in *Realms of Unknown Kings* (London: G. Richards, 1897), pp. 24-25.

5. Julie Anderson, lecture at Robert Schuller Institute on Church Growth, October 30, 1977.

6. *Letters from Lillian* (Springfield, Mo.: Division of Foreign Missions, Assemblies of God, 1983), p. 110.

7. Luci Swindoll, "Your Questions," *Solo,* vol. 2, 1984, p. 71.

8. Elisabeth Kübler-Ross, ed., *Death: The Final Stage of Growth* (Englewood Cliffs, N.J.: Prentice-Hal, 1975), p. 12.

5. ALTERNATIVES

1. Robert J. Havinghurst, *Developmental Tasks and Education,* 3rd ed. (White Plains, N.Y.: Longman, 1972), pp. 83-84.

2. U.S. Bureau of the Census, Current Population Reports, P-20, no. 389, *Marital Status and Living Arrangements: March, 1983* (Washington, D.C.: U.S. Government Printing Office, 1984), p. 3.

8. ATTITUDE-SHAPERS

1. Dietrich Bonhoeffer, *The Cost of Discipleship,* trans. Reginald H. Fuller (New York: Macmillan, 1960); *Prisoner for God: Letters and Papers from Prison,* ed. Eberhard Bethge (New York: Macmillan, 1954).

2. Allen Hadidian, *A Single Thought: God's Word on Singleness* (Chicago: Moody Press, 1981), pp. 88-89.

9. PAUL'S AGENDA

1. Susan Annette Muto, *Celebrating the Single Life* (New York: Doubleday, 1982), p. 106.

10. UNDERSTANDING THE SINGLE ADULT MALE

1. Kenneth L. Smith, *Learning to Be a Man* (Downers Grove: Inter Varsity Press, 1975), back cover.

2. Ken Druck, *The Secrets Men Keep* (New York: Doubleday, 1985), p. 33. See also James E. Kilgore, *The Intimate Man* (Nashville: Abingdon Press, 1984).

11. THE JABEZ SYNDROME

1. Barbara Sher, *Wishcraft: How to Get What You Really Want* (New York: Ballantine Books, 1983), p. 176.

2. Katherine Lackman, *Arkenstone,* March/April, 1981, p. 19.

12. SERVANTHOOD

1. Meta Rutter Pennock, ed., *Makers of Nursing History* (New York: Lakeside Publishers, 1940), p. 19.

2. *Letters from Lillian,* pp. 119-20.

3. Dorothy Clarke Wilson, *Stranger and Traveler: The Story of Dorothea Dix* (Boston: Little, Brown, 1975), p. 51.

13. ACCOUNTABILITY

1. Ginger Hutton, "Ginger Hutton: A Column," *Arizona Republic,* April 25, 1985, f-6.

2. Bobbie Reed, *Making the Most of Single Life* (St. Louis: Concordia Publishing House, 1980), p. 5.

3. Muto, *Celebrating the Single Life,* p. 72.

4. Alfred Armand Montapert, self-published manuscript.

BIBLIOGRAPHY

Baker, Yvonne G. *Successfully Single*. Denver: Accent Books, 1985.

Foster, Richard. *Money, Sex and Power*. New York: Harper & Row, 1985.

Hadidian, Allen. *A Single Thought*. Chicago: Moody Press, 1981.

Hansel, Tim. *Gotta Keep Dancin'*. Elgin, Ill.: David C. Cook, 1985.

Kushner, Harold S. *When All You've Ever Wanted Isn't Enough*. New York: Summit Books, 1986.

McAllaster, Elva. *Free to Be Single*. Chappaqua, N.Y.: Christian Herald, 1979.

Meredith, Don. *Who Says Get Married?* Nashville: Thomas Nelson, 1981.

Muto, Susan Annette. *Celebrating the Single Life: A Spirituality for Single Persons in Today's World*. New York: Doubleday, 1982.

Nouwen, Henri J. *The Way of the Heart*. New York: Ballantine Books, 1983.

Payne, Dorothy. *Singleness*. Philadelphia: Westminster Press, 1983.

Reed, Bobbie. *I Didn't Plan to Be a Single Parent*. St. Louis: Concordia Publishing House, 1981.

———. *Making the Most of Single Life*. St. Louis: Concordia Publishing House, 1980.

Sher, Barbara. *Wishcraft: How to Get What You Really Want*. New York: Ballantine Books, 1983.

Short, Ray E. *Sex, Dating and Love*. Minneapolis: Augsburg Publishing House, 1984.

———. *Sex, Love, or Infatuation: How Can I Really Know?* Minneapolis: Augsburg Publishing House, 1978.

Smedes, Lewis B. *Choices: Making Right Decisions in a Complex World*. New York: Harper & Row, 1986.

Smith, Harold Ivan. *I Wish Someone Understood My Divorce.* Minneapolis: Augsburg Publishing House, 1987.

———. *Life-Changing Answers to Depression.* Eugene, Ore.: Harvest House, 1985.

———. *Positively Single: Coming to Terms with the Single Life.* Wheaton, Ill.: Victor Books, 1986.

Smoke, Jim. *Living Beyond Divorce.* Eugene, Ore.: Harvest House, 1985.

Stevenson, Ruth. *Bible Readings for Singles.* Minneapolis: Augsburg Publishing House, 1980.